Encountering Illness

James Woodward

Encountering Illness

Voices in Pastoral and Theological Perspective

SCM PRESS LTD

0 334 02620 2

First published 1995
by SCM Press Ltd
9–17 St Albans Place, London N1 0NX

Typeset at The Spartan Press Ltd,
Lymington, Hants
and printed in Great Britain by
Mackays of Chatham, Kent

Contents

Acknowledgments

All learning is done in partnership and this particular expression of my present exploration into illness is no exception. Many of the ideas and feelings here have emerged through collaboration with a wide range of individuals and groups. The focus of this piece of writing is illness and it is my privilege to be a small part of that experience in a busy teaching hospital. Thanks to everyone who has made my encounter with illness so challenging and rewarding: patients, their families and friends; managers and politicians; doctors, nurses and all those people who make up the life of a hospital. These encounters have happened as part of a chaplaincy team, lay and ordained, women and men, paid and voluntary workers. This team in its variety and richness is a place of support, encouragement and engagement. Thanks to them all, past and present, but especially Renate Wilkinson, Barry Clark, Don Wrapson, Joan Griffin, Roy Brookstein, Roy Evans, Irene Bound and John Carlyle. Special thanks to our secretary, Kay Edwards, whose professionalism and patience supports our work.

Many of the ideas within the chapters have been discussed with a range of groups as part of formal and informal teaching. My Open University students helped broaden health perspectives and I am grateful to students from the University of Birmingham Medical School and the Queen Elizabeth College of Nursing for sharing in the process of continuous co-learning as we engaged together with the experience of illness. Our team work is enriched through links with the Queen's Theological College, Oscott College, the West Midlands Ministerial Training Scheme and the Department of Theology in the University of Birmingham. A small group of curates discussed dimensions of this project as part of their post-ordination training: James Curry, Nigel Jones and Bill Moore. Chapter 8 began its life as a lecture to the John Young Foundation in Stafford and other ideas have been tested out with my national chaplaincy colleagues through my editorship of the Journal of Health Care Chaplaincy.

Finally, a number of friends gave time to final drafts and improved the text through their responses: Mark Pryce, Beaumont Stevenson, Ronald Coppin, Jo Harries, Stephen Pattison, Peter Harvey and Leslie Houlden. I have no hesitation in dedicating it to Leslie who has given me over fifteen years of friendship and support, encouraging me in theological study. His integrity and honesty are an important inspiration for my work and exploration.

Introduction

This book concerns the human encounter with the realities of illness. This is a complex subject, for illnesses are not the discrete, precisely defined entities that one might suppose. The causes of illness and what makes for health depend on such a range of factors that any encounter with the voices of illness will be, inevitably, a challenge; a struggle to understand, hear and connect with this ambiguous and paradoxical reality. The book will attempt to listen to the voices of illness and in that encounter face the experiences and questions of individuals and groups. It is then a discourse of discovery; a meeting and connecting that is open-ended and never-ending. My aim is not to provide a text-book that describes and controls the experiences around illness but to invite the reader into a deeper encounter with the wide range of voices here audible in the text. Honesty and realism are important guiding principles in this encounter. In this sense, this act of writing is, like most writing, an act of therapy. I want to be honest about what I believe to be true, and open to the challenges and questions that continue to perplex, irritate and pain me. So, this is a book arising from my own attention to the voices of illness.

The chapters that follow are also a work of pastoral and practical theology. For they attempt to put the encounter and experience into pastoral and theological perspective. There is at work here an important theological method which found its liberating birth in my editing of *Embracing the Chaos, Theological Responses to AIDS*. This method is about holding together experience and tradition, practice and theory as interdependent realities that need to engage and connect with each other within the living tradition of the Christian faith. This dynamic and holistic approach should involve the whole person and his or her community as it holds together and fosters a dialogue between spiritual experience and theological knowledge or tradition. So it follows that there are two important dimensions to the process of putting the encounters into some kind of pastoral and theological perspective. The first is the actual encounter with illness. It is a matter of listening to those who experience illness from a number of perspectives and attending closely to *their* questions and agendas. Their stories both value and affirm experience as a rich resource for learning. Part of being a Christian is to share our life stories, to reflect upon them in the light of faith and in reflecting, integrate them into our living and growing. While some of the experiences described here are drawn from a variety of other sources, most come from my own pastoral ministry within the context of a large teaching hospital. Certain names and situations have been changed to protect confidentiality.

Above all, careful attention has to be paid to the way in which experience is used. So often in the appropriation of experience there can be a kind of hijacking, an abuse of the preciousness of what is shared. The experiences presented here are offered in the realization that what is given in the sharing is profound, involving a struggle with the heart of human existence, the nature of God and the process of salvation. In all this process one needs to be conscious of the reality of control and power in the process of learning.

It would be impossible and even undesirable to impose too much order on the experience or on the questions that emerge from asking ourselves 'What is illness?' Rather, those involved in pastoral care reflecting on experience need to beware of identifying with a medical model of care that perceives the 'problem' and then controls a strategy to identify and solve it. This approach to pastoral theology will always be too restricted, and it fails to understand the complex nature of experience. There is no such thing as 'neutral experience'; as the words take shape to articulate it, a process of interpretation takes place in the choice of words, images, feelings and facts. There is a dynamic relationship between the objective and subjective in the articulation of experience.

This writing is a piece of practical and pastoral theology. At the heart of its understanding of the vocation of the pastor lies the belief that the Christian must be suspicious of all models of reality for they only represent part of that reality. The Christian tradition, viewed from one perspective, is a continual process of making and breaking the models that can become idols in our thinking and practice; and they change anyway, try as we may to freeze them. This is why the interactive process undergirding this work is important and why the results will always be partial, incomplete and open-ended. To prevent these models or frameworks from becoming idols they need to be opened up and evaluated in the light of the gospel, God and the life of the Christian community. There is an inevitable eschatological dimension in this sort of project, in so far as it represents experience that has been transformed and transfigured as one particular pastor struggles with the mystery on the way to a fulfilment as yet unfinished. This process goes beyond schemata. This work is about humanity that moves into mystery and it affirms a struggle with ambiguity and paradox that leaves the theologian searching for words; struggling to know what to say. This is part of what it means to live by faith, for within this process none of us knows what we shall become. In this perspective we should resist the movement that impels so much of modern spirituality to go psychological, for in that movement there is often uncritical allegiance to an ideology that replaces paradox with the security of certainty and belief. The encounter with illness needs to be authentic, that is, as free from any kind of ideology as possible, whether psychological or theological. At root, there needs to be the simplicity of persons listening to each other, and all else needs to be seen as provisional.

The raw experience of encountering illness, however, is not enough. A vital element in helping people to understand the implications of the gospel is the need to ensure that this experience is consciously reflected upon in the light of our faith. Historically, tradition has been understood as that which is contained normatively in scripture and the experience of the church. At its core is the nature of God and the relationship of God to creation. Tradition, however, has always been and will always be dynamic, changing and developing, and this dynamic quality is often a cause of anxiety and conflict. It is my concern here to ask what dimensions of the encounter with illness affirm tradition and what dimensions may challenge aspects of tradition, and indeed contribute to its developing and changing quality. It is, then, not just ourselves who learn from this encounter. There may also be learning to be done by our theological tradition. Of course tradition cannot depend only on individual experience, because it is above all something that is corporately experienced in our common Christian life and our worship. This is why this exploration is tentative. It affirms that there is, to begin with, a personal discovery; the learning is a reflecting on experience and the authority is vested primarily in the process of growth in the one who listens and encounters. This has implications for models of ministry and for our understanding of human nature and the learning process. In this sense, I believe that all of life is intrinsically theological. This assertion has been confirmed by my own encounter with illness. For these are the theological questions that individuals and groups most ask: Where did we come from and why are we here? (creation). What is the purpose of human existence? (teleology). What would attaining perfection mean and what would change the situation? (salvation). In what or in whom do we put our trust and what can we dare to hope for? (eschatology).

Theology is not a set of principles or concepts to be somehow put into practice, nor is it a history to be seen as binding. It is a way of exploring our world and requires our total involvement: heart and mind; thought and action; private and corporate. I want to know more about the God who is love and justice and about how that God, our God, is to be discerned in event and story, in language and soil. To do this I must start with the stories of those I encounter and allow that encounter to help shape my theology. Theologizing becomes a very local affair, closely related to the particular. In this important sense experience ought to play its part in shaping the form and the content of theology. The stories themselves become part of the living, enabling and empowering tradition of the church. This understanding of theology coheres with our understanding that all theological statements are provisional: they are bound in time and place, to age and culture. As Christian communities engaging with our world we need to ask why so much theology seems remote and useless and why many find other frames of reference so much more illuminating for their journey – or manage without such frames altogether. Propositions about God are always partial and provisional because the nature of God as perceived by fallible human beings is bound to change and adapt. Even if we think in terms of revelation by God, the medium is still our changing human perception of the divine mystery. Our perceptions and apprehensions are partial: music in the process of being performed and written, with all the risks, uncertainties and mistakes that adventure entails.

This piece of writing relates, in part then, to a wider debate about the nature of theology as a language of truth. Meanings are important and the theme running through this book is 'What is the meaning of illness?' The questions are: Is that meaning fixed, and what is the method by which truth in these matters is apprehended? What kind of discourse will enable the reader to journey through this complex terrain? For the subject matter of illness there are many languages that contribute to our experience: the languages of medicine, surgery, health promotion, therapy or spirituality. I do not wish to be confined to any particular language, approach or story. The purpose is to explore what the encounter with illness means, what can be affirmed with certainty and what cannot.

I join with others in a call to recover theology as a discipline that is exploratory which will help people to live openly and gloriously. This is why pastoral theology is a vital discipline, process and tool for the task in recovering an enlivening link between faith and life. The voices represented here should help us to be both explorers and map-makers in that exploration.

Using this theological method the overriding aim is to empower growth and wholeness. My concern is to ask continually what sort of theological map or framework will enable the community to make sense of experience and unfold Christian meaning in and through that experience. The theology in *Encountering Illness* is discovered in a questioning journey into the reality of this vital feature of human life.

The ten chapters that follow will take a number of different dimensions of the encounter with illness and explore the experience in the light of this theological method. I hope that you will be enriched and challenged by your encounter with illness through these chapters. The subject matter of each of them is self-explanatory. There are no footnotes but I have included in the appendix some of my source material and suggestions for further reading.

Pain, Loss and Anxiety:

Exploring human existence in the light of illness

- **Jayne**

I remember the preparation and journey into the hospital in very particular detail. My perceptions were heightened as my husband helped me pack my bag, reread the instructions the hospital had sent us and planned the route. What would the traffic be like at that time of the morning? Should I have some breakfast? Have I remembered to leave my husband all the practical things necessary for his survival!? When the day came, and it came very slowly because I found it difficult to sleep, I found it difficult to eat anything but managed a cup of tea and we set off early on our journey. The traffic wasn't bad and we arrived at the hospital at just before 9.00 am. The worst thing was, of course, that we could not park. We drove round and round trying to find a space but without success – my husband was patient but I could feel that we were both getting anxious about the time. Eventually he decided to drop me off at the main entrance and park the car off the hospital site. I waited in the entrance for him with a couple of other people. One old chap was sitting in the corner smoking and another woman, of about my age, looked so pale and had obviously been crying. I wanted to speak to her but was afraid of what had upset her. Time passed slowly. I watched ambulances pull in and deliver all kinds of different people, in wheel chairs and on stretchers, to the hospital doors. Eventually my husband turned up looking very hot and breathless. He had parked the car up near the university and ran down to the hospital. Suddenly, as I caught his eye, I felt a sense of his vulnerability – he looked older and I could tell how worried he was. We were greeted kindly by a hospital volunteer who took us to wait in the Registration Office, so we could get our paperwork sorted out. As I sat there looking around on an uncomfortable chair I wondered what the next few days would bring, and I realized how much I hated hospitals and how much I feared what might happen to me.

- **Linda**

My name is Linda and I come to the hospital three times a week for renal dialysis. I travel into Birmingham from Hereford which can be long and rather tedious but is always made better by the cheerful hospital car driver who tells me all about his life and adventures. You get used to having kidney problems after a while and there is a kind of familiarity with all the test procedures and especially with the process of dialysis, with all those tubes and things. I used to feel angry and disappointed about the problems that I have had but I don't really bother about those now – I take each day as it comes and make the best of what I've got. I like the hospital – I think I probably know more about some of the nurses than their parents do! They are kind, always ready to help and sometimes very loving. But above all, what I like about the hospital is this chapel where I am sitting now, with its simple cross. It's peaceful and quiet. I'm not really very Christian and all that but I like coming here – it feels as if this place is the heart of this busy hospital. I have been to one or two of the services and in a way they reflect the helping and loving and sharing that Christianity goes on about and I have experienced here over the last four years.

- **Jonathan**

I am lying at home waiting for the nurse to come and sort me out. I chose to die at home even though I live on my own and sometimes am afraid of having so much of my own company. The GP and the district nurse have been marvellous really, in helping me to die in the way that I want. They explain the treatment to me carefully and sensitively, and I have a sense of being in charge of my treatment, though totally out of control of the situation! There are lots of positives about the ways in which people help and support me but I want to tell you some of the negatives. The first frustration is that often I feel I am made into a problem who is a person rather than a person who happens to have a problem. I don't know how much information I need to know to die well; to be honest, I can't remember half of the stuff that is told to me – some of those tablets have extraordinary funny names! The doctor is good but I do feel for him. I think that being a doctor is one of the most difficult jobs in the whole world; we deprive the poor people of their sleep and heap on them all kinds of expectations and demands. So I guess it isn't surprising that it feels that his presence can be distant and technical and cold. Perhaps it's too costly to be human? So I understand the distance and I understand the need for technical excellence but I wonder where the doctor is in all this and what his job does to him as a person.

• Michael

My name is Michael and I'm lying in the middle of a large Nightingale Ward where I've been a patient for the last ten days. It's a large busy medical ward and I'm undergoing a number of tests and investigations – nobody seems to know what on earth is happening to me at the moment. My overwhelming impression of being here is the activity and the noise. These excellent, professional people say, in so many different ways, that they are busy; that there is no time; that there is always a job to be done. I find efficiency both wonderful and frightening at the same time. Sometimes I would really like to talk to one of them but they use all kinds of things to prevent themselves from getting drawn into my own funny little world of concern, fear and anxiety. I hate waiting, and the most difficult thing for me is living and coping with the uncertainty of all this. I wonder if they really know what's wrong and are not telling me? And what are they going to do to find out – how many more tests will they need to take? In some ways I would rather have the diagnosis, even if it's really bad, just to be sure of where I stand. Of course, it is not all bad. There are people who get themselves involved in a way that is personal – that helps and, perhaps, even heals. The cleaner has a way of kind of caring about me in the way that she clears my table and comments on my pyjamas! In a strange way, I think that the nurses have become kind of attached to me and I feel that I belong here. I hope that I don't have to belong here long and that they find out soon.

• **Sarah**

My name is Sarah and I've been laid up at home for a few months now following a period of stay in hospital. I injured my back by falling off a ladder – don't ask me how I managed to get into that pickle! The thing that strikes me about my disability is that it has produced in me an amazing greater level of awareness. It has given me a clarity about the relationships that I have in all their ambiguity and paradoxes. But above all, at last, after 45 years there are endless things that I have taken for granted that I can now see in such a different light. The colour in the sky, some of the pictures around the house, the wood in the trees in the garden, the quality of a good cup of tea and the small act of care showed through holding my hand or mopping my brow; these are wonderful gifts and I feel thankful for this greater awareness – life won't ever be the same again.

★

There is a curious level of acceptance that permeates each of the voices in the above paragraphs. One wonders how the different people might answer the question, 'What is illness?' In a way the question needs no answer for we all know what illness is. We all become ill and will all be ill at some stage of our lives. In this sense, illness is a natural process – it is a biological response to something going wrong and it is part of our biology. While the voices here strike us as painful and even tragic, they also demonstrate an acceptance of the inevitability and naturalness of their illness.

People cope with illness in so many different ways. Some
people manage to disregard it and to maintain a level of activity
in the midst of it. Others are submerged. These different levels
of attitude depend in part on our temperament and in part on
our awareness of normality. Linda copes with her level of
disability by taking it and, as far as she is able, integrating it into
her routine; she makes the best of what she's got! Sarah delights
in the intensity of her greater awareness of people and
situations, while Michael, Jonathan and Jayne have to deal with
a whole variety of emotions.

The first lesson that we are taught by the voices of Jayne,
Linda, Jonathan, Michael and Sarah is that illness faces us with
the challenging reality that there are limits to our knowledge.
Medical knowledge has expanded vastly in recent years. This
modern expansion had its birth in the 1940s and continued
throughout the 1950s and the following decades, to provide a
huge range of therapies for all kinds of serious illnesses;
antibiotics and steroids, anti-cancer drugs and surgery, pain
control drugs and even the ability of surgeons to replace whole
organs of the body. This has resulted in an expansion of
expectations on the part of both patients and doctors. How far
do we now assume that all illness can be cured? Do we not all
live with an expectation of 'limited immortality' as we harbour
the sense that nothing should go wrong with our bodies in seven
and a half decades that cannot be rectified? Illness, however,
tells us that medical science is not all-knowing and that there
continue to be huge gaps in our knowledge. There may be
limited knowledge about the illness, or indeed the treatment.
Michael's doctors may never be able to diagnose successfully
what the problem is with him. Of course, in some cases the
cause of an illness is obvious; but in others it is not clear, and on
the strength of the information available to the doctor it may be
hard to tell whether or not the condition is serious. Many
feelings of being unwell tend to disappear of their own accord
and sometimes without their underlying basis ever being
known.

The feeling that is implicit in many of the voices is that of
anxiety, an unpleasant emotion aroused by the events of illness

which are perceived to be a threat to human health and wellbeing. We are told that fear is aroused by a sense of local threat from which the victim feels an impulse to flee, whereas anxiety is typically aroused by unknown or unintelligible stimuli. Illness often seems mysterious to the one who suffers it, even if it is well understood scientifically. Existentialists describe anxiety as a fear of non-being, and this can imply not only death, but also a sense of meaninglessness and a sense of guilt that seem to foreshadow death.

The source of anxiety for Jayne is the fear of being separated from others, particularly her husband, who are felt to provide security for her and to depend on her. We have all had the experience of the anxiety that results from the threat of separation from our parents. In some ways anxiety is aroused not only by risks to survival, but also by real or imagined risks to our sense of personal identity as accorded to us by family and community. We develop a whole range of defence mechanisms to restrain anxiety, or keep it from awareness, but the mechanisms do not abolish it. Anxiety is an emotion which (particularly if it is unrecognized) spreads as if by contagion. It is, however, an essential part of the human condition and can never be eliminated, and it can be turned to creative use.

The main factor in our encounter with the voices in this chapter is that they point to the importance of the personal dimension in the treatment of patients. This means in practice a deliberate and compassionate sharing of the burden, so as to lessen the weight. It means sensitivity to the realities of the situation in all their complexity, rawness and unresolvedness. Too often there is a tendency to relieve the anxiety in ways that underplay its reality. The doctor can easily turn to drug therapy to relieve anxiety or depression. The temptation for the nurse or helper is to give a hasty reassurance that fails to engage with the person and his or her feelings.

There is here a Christian ethical interest in highlighting the proposition that, on moral grounds as well as for its therapeutic value, health care ought to resource this personal dimension to the encounter with the patient and his or her illness. There is no substitute for this quality of care and the doctor or the nurse or the therapist, with all their technical excellence, can fail to be truly personal (let alone vulnerable) in responding to another's story and needs.

There is, as we have noticed, a surprising, even perplexing, accepting quality in the voices we attend to. Is it not surprising the way people, whom society normally expects to 'stand up for themselves', readily take on a passive role when they are in a hospital situation? They give in and are ready to be passive in a variety of ways. Jonathan looks to the nurse to sort him out and hopes the doctor will give him the answers to his questions. Sarah and Linda show courage and fortitude in their adversity and manage to assert some control over their passivity. Perhaps here too there is a dimension of Christian ethics: A 'cross-derived' moral and spiritual emphasis. We note the prominence of Jesus' passivity in the passion story as told in the Gospel of Mark. These factors identified as having Christian significance ultimately go back to the Christ-centred character of Christianity. The theological truth is that the passivity and pain and sheer raw vulnerability of the cross as a personal experience speak to the human condition in the hospital. What kind of language might help people to articulate this passivity and vulnerability, a sharing in what may look like a community of suffering? For Linda the focus of the chapel, the plain wooden cross, speaks powerfully. She searches for a language to help her describe and make sense of her condition. From my perspective, this theological dimension to the encounter with illness feels fundamental and essential to a containing and embracing of human existence in the light of the experience of pain, loss and anxiety. In this sense, Christianity is a religion whose meaning and concept are of such a character that it is wholly appropriate for it to be an essential element in hospitals. This assertion emerges straight out of the agenda set by this encounter with human pain and loss.

The quality of the voices described here lies in the honesty of the unease and anxiety that are experienced and articulated. There is a kind of terror, weariness and intensity about human existence in the light of illness. Some people have described themselves, on reflection in the light of their illness, as being only partly alive. But in another way, their illness has given them the opportunity to live more deeply, to see new things, to discover a dimension to their living that had remained, to that time, hidden or untouched. There is a theological and religious agenda here, if it is true that the purpose of religion is the creation of new life and the regeneration of energy in the light of faith in Christ. There is then, or can be, in the experience of illness, both a theological experience of redemption and an emotional experience of healing. Some would not wish to give this any theological language or significance but it seems that the inherent reality of the cross is being reenacted as a person comes to a new awareness of what is important; what is worth living for and dying for. Anxiety, therefore, may be a friend rather than an enemy in that the qualities of anxiety may grasp people in a way that allows them to live more fully and deeply. Perhaps this is the reality which Linda describes. It is a rediscovery of the self in the light of something that lies beneath and beyond human comprehension but is glimpsed in a variety of encounters. It is a kind of confrontation with God.

From a theological point of view any discussion of the creative anxiety of the cross can usefully include the contribution of Paul Tillich in his book *The Courage to Be*. He perceived certain types of anxieties as being inescapable: to avoid them is to lose one's humanity. The courage to take this inescapable anxiety upon oneself assumes three main forms: the courage to be as a part of a larger whole, the courage to stand alone, the courage to accept the fact that humankind is carried by the creative power of being in which every creature participates. Tillich argues that the neurotic person is one who is more highly sensitive to the threat of self-destruction, of non-being. This person retires to a castle and defends it with all means of psychological resistance against attack, either from reality or from the pastor. The neurotic handling of anxiety becomes evident as the inability to take one's existential anxiety upon oneself.

This anxiety, from the Christian perspective, cannot be borne alone. It serves to make confrontation with God all the more imperative. The impending necessity of such a cross thrusts humankind into the very presence of God. The person's dependence upon the providence of God, one's finite weakness manifest in the anxiety of creatureliness, the pressure of the sense of estrangement in grief, the awareness of sin and the need for liberation from it – all these come to a kind of crescendo of sheer terror, pain, loss and anxiety in the face of illness, which might be described as a kind of holy dread – if perceived in the light of God. This is where existence is changed, as it takes on a different shape in the light of illness.

2

Waiting, Watching and Hoping:

Exploring the perspectives of relatives and friends

- **Sandra**

I arrived at the Out Patients Department of a large London hospital with my friend who had a 1.30 pm appointment. The receptionist, a pleasant young man, seemed faintly surprised to see us both an hour early, consulted his computer and pointed to a chair. Already a trickle of patients had found their way through the confusion of buildings and corridors and were standing, silent and hopeful, by a now empty reception desk. There was a group of people waiting by the desk, mainly elderly people, who stood holding their letters towards the empty reception desk with expressions of hopefulness and resignation, as they were waiting for something to which they had become accustomed.

'Sit down! over there! until the receptionist comes!' The order came from a person in a green overall walking briskly across the room. I wondered how much the word, 'sorry' or 'please', cost the person?

1.30 pm came and went. 1.45 pm came and went. The room now held around thirty people. Human beings in an unusual state of vulnerability, largely elderly, some foreign, waiting for the confirmation of their fears, the lifting of their dread. I chatted with my friend but felt overwhelmed by her rising sense of anxiety and insecurity. I searched within myself to find words of comfort and reassurance. Reading through the literature I came across the *Patients' Charter* which informed us that if the appointment was not kept within thirty minutes, 'Patients will receive an explanation and indication of how long they will have to wait'. No explanation came to any of us. An hour after my friend's appointment time I asked the receptionist for one. He greeted this advocacy on my part with an air of faint surprise and said that he *thought* that the consultant would be coming soon. 'It is amazing how many people never turn up for an appointment', he said.

'Sit down!' commanded another overalled person. 'It's not your turn, love!' What were we, this small bundle of worried people, being given orders rather than service, condescension rather than courtesy? Certainly we were not clients. I began to feel remarkably like a cow waiting hopefully with its herd to be milked. We had become objects. We had been named 'patients' because our function was passively to exercise patience.

I wondered how single parents managed, those with dependent relatives, in relation to demanding employers. Still, my friend had no word of explanation, let alone an apology. Once she was half undressed, the consultant appeared shadowed by two students. He was efficient, sympathetic, speedy. The interview lasted ten minutes. On my way out with my friend past the rows of those still waiting, patient as monuments, I asked a green overalled figure whether it was usual for appointments to run an hour and a half late. She looked at me with great reproof. 'He has been operating', she said. It was, of course, however impressive, no answer.

• Patricia and Colin

We are a married couple in our middle years, both teachers with busy and demanding posts in secondary education. Patricia's mother is in her eighties and struggling with ill-health. At the moment she is in the local elderly care ward in the General Hospital. It is the first time Elizabeth, our mother, has been away from her home in her life and all kinds of things surprise us.

Of course, the staff here are helpful, kind and concerned. Despite this I couldn't escape the sense that Elizabeth was in an institution with its depersonalization and lack of choice. There is so little space; everything happens at her bedside as she is stripped of everything that marks her identity and individuality. There was the shocking experience for Colin of seeing his mother-in-law's nakedness and loss of dignity. She had to fit into the routine of the ward – meals, getting in and out of bed. The worst imposition was the lack of control over the lights on the ward which were switched off at an early hour. It felt like a warehouse for all these people. Amidst the routine, the tablets, doctor's round and the nurses' tasks, we were pained to know where our mother was in all this. We didn't want to make a fuss and wondered how much of all this was an inevitable part of a hospital's work.

• Isobel

My husband, Humphrey, is lying in an intensive care bed in hospital. He has had a brain haemorrhage and is battling with acute failure of his kidneys. He is unconscious and has not given any indication that he knows I am with him. His bed is surrounded with machinery and there must be over twenty tubes and leads from his body.

The consultant is clear and calm. He tells me that my husband's life is in the balance and the health care team are battling to understand what is going on with the systems and functions of his body. I am in shock. I can't sleep and don't feel like eating. The tests are endless.

The ward sister takes me to one side three days later and tells me that she doesn't feel that things are going well, and had I thought about what I would do if he didn't recover? Two hours later the consultant tells me in his calm voice that there is no change and they are doing all that they can. What is the truth? Who am I to believe?

There is, of course, a battle and struggle going on inside me. Part of me prays and hopes that my dearest husband will live and we can do all the things we had planned for retirement. Another part of me thinks that he has no hope, and even if he does live what sort of life might he have? What kind of brain damage might he have to live with? I feel guilty at the thought that I hope he might die so that I know where I stand on all this.

I hate the uncertainty, the unknowing, the swings and changes of all this. The thought of the loss of this man is so impossible to contemplate: he is everything to me – my reason for living. Time has never passed by so slowly.

• Hanif

Hanif is a young Asian man who has come to visit his grandmother in hospital. She is about to have radical surgery to take out a tumour from her womb. While they are talking the doctor's round appears and the consultant, unable to make himself understood, asks Hanif to act as interpreter. Hanif finds himself very involved both in his grandmother's distress and the intimate details of the surgery. He is shocked at how 'matter of fact' it all appears to the surgeon and is angry at how his grandmother is treated, in what appears to him as an offhand manner because her English is so poor.

• Elizabeth

I am the sister of Jessica who has been in hospital for many weeks now. I visit her daily and the hospital has become part of my routine, part of my life. I know about hospitals; I retired from the nursing staff ten years ago after forty years' service. All around is change and I feel this in all sorts of ways. I don't feel that it is easy not to be in control and it's interesting to watch the way people engage, especially the nursing staff. Perhaps this is my distress but I don't think that the nurses observe what is going on these days. If only they would look beyond the tasks to find out about feelings: to observe, communicate and listen to what is told, how it is told and why it is told. This is the secret, and it is then, and only then, that care will become meaningful. It's very difficult not to appear as a judge of all you survey, but if only we could take care in doing those little tasks and pay attention to the person: it is an art and a science.

★

There are some very important insights to be listened to and to engage with coming from those who stand on the margins of the experience of illness and observe. Some of the issues that are raised through our encounter with the stories above, focus on respect, dignity, privacy and informed choice. All health care professionals, and indeed patients, need to understand why situations are not treated with with as much sensitivity as they might be. Recognizing people's dignity means listening to their views. Thus our encounter with Hanif and his grandmother shows us that the care team were unable to engage because they failed to understand the differences arising from culture and role, not to speak of matters of gender, class, age and race. Elizabeth asks the nurse to treat the individual as a person and not just an illness, so that the wider human reality is taken into consideration. Too often people are discussed as if they were inanimate objects, tasks to be performed; not people in all their complexity.

The best kind of care works when those involved are truly engaged in the situation. This means employing human skills of empathy, listening, being alert and putting sensitivity into practice by recognizing and responding to a range of needs. This means that the individual's wishes and choices, their view of the world and understanding of the hospital are taken into consideration. Emotions, such as anxiety, fear, delight, confusion and pain need to be encompassed and embraced. This has a positive aspect in so far as the individual circumstances might be used positively to develop care. Often patients have amazing inner strengths, beliefs and attitudes which can be used creatively and positively. Above all, what the patient deserves is that the professional carers, who may be feeling stressed, do not take their emotions out on him or her or impose their own views or judgments.

Dignity is a fundamental human requirement focussing on basic needs such as dress and clothing, toileting, having choice in how one is named, maintaining a particular culture, lifestyle or dietary requirement: above all being treated as a human being and given value. Hospitals in particular need to look at their culture and how far they demand unnecessary conformity of those who receive care. Often the hospital can be perceived as a 'do as you're told culture'. Dignity means that a person is shown respect, that they are not stereotyped and that their whole person, their values, issues and concerns are listened to, heard, and responded to. This is, in part, about giving the patient some kind of control and involving him or her as an active participant in the process of healing and wholeness.

Privacy and respect are values that, while in some respects obvious, are often not taken into consideration in a range of situations. This is particularly true for people of other cultural traditions. If there is doubt, then the rule must be to allow the patient to inform the carer whose own task is to ask the patient about wants and needs. These needs focus again around the human values of sensitivity, courtesy and common decency. It is also necessary to attend to the environment with regard to factors like light, noise and colour. Partnership works where there is shared care and power is equal, where there is a mutual acceptance of values and open communication. Autonomy is maintained when there is participation in the management process and information is adequate, appropriate and accessible. There needs to be an ownership of this process so that wherever possible Hanif's grandmother, Elizabeth, and Patricia and Colin's mother can have some freedom through the maintenance of their independence.

The gospel tells us that Jesus identifies himself in a particular way with the poor, the sick and the imprisoned. Jesus gives emphasis to the truth that it is his followers' hands that are used for his work of healing. So Jesus is at one with both the healed and the healer, the victim and the carer. John V. Taylor's concept of the Holy Spirit as the go-between God who is knowable in the relationships between people is of vital importance here. The heart of this doctrine tells us that in all the relationships which the individual has with all the people trying to help – the family, doctors and therapists – the Holy Spirit is present and active in all their work.

The Spirit is particularly at work around waiting, watching and hoping. This theme is particularly illuminated theologically by the words of Jesus in the garden of Gethsemane: 'Watch with me.' The word *watch* says many things on different levels, all of importance to us: there is both a kind of vigilance and a kind of guarding. The relatives and friends know that care and relationship are ultimately to do with attentiveness to the person in all their vulnerability and distress. They are close to those they love; and begin to understand what kind of pain the patient experiences.

These case studies show us that patients need warmth and friendship as well as technical care. They need support and companionship. We who watch need to be aware of what it feels like to be ill: to be painfully separated from the person that you were, to be separated from loves and responsibilities. Pastoral care has to learn to feel 'with' patients, without feeling like them. Such attitudes give substance to the sense of relationships in which the role of the Spirit of God is experienced as a reality. This coming close transforms people's lives. There is a still deeper level at which the words 'watch with me' are significant. Our learning of skills and techniques and our attempt to understand mental suffering and loneliness, and to pass on what we have learnt, are not the whole of the matter. However much we can ease distress, however much we can help patients to find a new meaning in what is happening, there will always be the place where we have to stop and accept that we are really helpless. This is what our relatives and friends teach us through their stories above. 'Watch with me' means, above all, just being there.

There can be no hope without the recognition by all concerned that this part of the patient's experience is very hard. The problems and difficulties need to be faced honestly: the anxiety, the depression, the weakness, the dependence and the isolation from other people's lives and activity. Only the acceptance of the facts of loss and darkness and the possibility of death in all their negativity makes for the creative hope of resurrection, of new birth, of light beyond the darkness.

The christological dimension, pointing us to models in the life of Jesus, adds other aspect to our shared approach. Christ may be seen as present in symbols and sacraments of all kinds. We may have in mind the giving of a cup of cold water (Mark

9.41) and the washing of the disciples' feet (John 13.1–15).
Comparable acts of relatives and friends will speak silently to
the patient about love. In the relationships between the patient
and loved ones in speech and act, there is a basis of trust and
respect in which something very important is happening.

There are, of course, all kinds of questions and issues raised
by relatives and friends, above all those of why and how.
Dennis Potter, the playwright, has spoken about the freedom of
the human being as something being given. At the time of an
interview with Mary Craig he was disabled by a painful and rare
form of arthritic disease. He said, 'I have the sense that the
world is made every day, second by second, minute by minute,
and we, living in this world, give back some of that initial gift,
minute by minute, second by second; that even the most trivial
choice can have awesome consequences; that we choose to live
in relation to other people in a continual tension of choice: that
the choice has its origin in a loving creation, and that loving
creation is in continual battle and tension with, and in obvious
opposition to the misery, cruelty and crudity of an imperfect
world that we have to endure and live in and do battle with.'

3

Myths, Meanings and Re-evaluations:

Exploring coping mechanisms in illness

- **Jane**

  Jane is a 46 year-old woman who has been admitted into hospital for a course of chemotherapy to treat lung cancer. Doctors suspect that she may have secondary deposits of cancer in her liver. While her long-term prognosis is not good they hope to halt the spread of the disease and relieve some physical pain. Jane had a radical mastectomy four years ago. She is divorced and has remarried very happily, with two children from her first marriage aged 24 and 22, and three children from her second marriage aged 11, 9, and 4. She is a strong energetic woman, whose family are heavily dependent upon her.

- **Robert**

  Robert is an elderly gentleman who collapsed in Harborne High Street and was admitted on to a very busy medical ward. After seven days of tests, a consultant surgeon arrives to inform him that he has an inoperable tumour. He asks the domestic to call for a chaplain. He shares his story with great courage. His wife died forty years ago to leave him to bring up two young daughters. Twelve years ago one daughter died of cancer. Since then he has cared for his elderly mother who died earlier in the year aged 92. He holds the chaplain's hand and says calmly, 'I'm not afraid of dying but I'm scared stiff of going home on my own – I'm absolutely alone.'

• Michael

Michael is a divorced 34 year-old who has been given a diagnosis of terminal cancer. He becomes increasingly withdrawn and, although he is compliant with the ward routine, he refuses to engage with any offer to talk the matter through, however informally it is offered.

The nursing team refer him to a Macmillan nurse. When she arrives, Michael says firmly, 'I don't need you. I am getting better. Please go away.'

• Margaret

Mrs Roberts is a 52 year-old married woman with three grown up children, aged 32, 28 and 27. She is a deputy headmistress at a local junior school and a leading light in the local amateur dramatics society. She had a hysterectomy two years ago and is in hospital for a course of chemotherapy to treat her cancer. Her prognosis is good. It takes the staff nurse two hours to take her details for the ward records because Margaret asks a whole series of questions about the symptoms of her cancer and the likelihood of her cure. She wants to know in precise detail the nature of chemotherapy and seems concerned, not with whether the chemotherapy will be successful, but whether the cancer will come back after she has been cured. She also explores with the staff nurse the possibility of alternative therapy. As the staff nurse makes her excuses to leave, Margaret asks 'Why has this happened to me?'

• Janet

Each morning Janet busies herself with setting her bedside cabinet in order and making the bed in her ward area. She then proceeds to help the domestic with the tea and encourages each of the three patients in her area to get up and assists them in washing. She's busy, very active and always enthusiastic and optimistic. She is determined not to let the cancer get the better of her and her advice to her neighbours is 'don't dwell on your illness – don't let it get you!'

★

The sheer vulnerability and fragility of life marks these lives out as a reminder to us of the possibility of illness for any of us at any time. Jane's story is a reminder of how often women bear the weight of responsibility for children within the family. Her family are heavily dependent upon her and she needs them: there is a sense in which she believes that she can't die because she is needed. There is a deep sense of a will that wants to live. This may have a significantly positive affect upon her prognosis. There is also a sense from Jane's story that she has had some experience in coming to terms with loss through the break-up of her first marriage. She knows through this experience of loss that good can come out of bad. With so much to live for there is a degree of anger as she wonders what place God might have in the onset of cancer.

It is the deep sense of loneliness that dominates our encounter with Robert. He has coped stoically with the role of carer and knows the deep pain of loss and how death transforms the geography of human life. For one that has been able to give out so much to others, it may be difficult to adapt to the vulnerability of receiving help.

There is an inevitable loneliness to all illness and Robert bears eloquent witness to this. The encounter with Michael may elicit different responses. Some may think that he lacks the substance to face reality; others that his denial is an entirely appropriate shutting out of the prospect of pain. Self-absorption that refuses help seems wholly understandable. There is an energy about both Margaret's and Janet's engagement with their cancer that takes a different shape. Margaret needs to know and expresses her fear through an attempt to exercise control over her situation. Janet's activity could be viewed as either diversion from the uncertainty and pain of her cancer, or more positively, her refusal to allow self-absorption and the illness to dominate her horizons. Either way, both of these non-compliant patients present particular challenges for a structured caring process that does not easily accommodate individuality.

We all assume that we are safe from threat and operate with an illusion of invulnerability. It is others who are victims of disease, crime and accidents. So when faced with a diagnosis that is catastrophic, people go through a complex process of re-evaluation and appraisal. This is described by psychologists as a person's survival schema. This re-evaluation is a process by which the individual selects, filters and interprets the information that is heard. A process of adjustment takes place as the individual takes a view of the diagnosis that is provided, gathers perceptions about his or her own control in the light of that diagnosis, and proceeds to work out what kind of life is possible in the light of the information that has been given. A patient's pattern of thought, feelings and behaviour associated with these re-evaluations represents a loose style of adjustment which can then be developed. This is a coping mechanism or an adjustment style.

Janet's adjustment style might be described as a fighting spirit. She sees the cancer as a challenge and attempts to exert control over all that it means to her. She seems to indicate that she is able to be optimistic in the light of all that has happened to her. For her it is a challenge to be overcome. She has gained as much information as possible about the disease and aims to take an active role in recovering; but above all, she will attempt to live as normally as possible. Typical statements from others demonstrating this fighting spirit might be: 'I don't dwell on my illness' or (as Janet says by her activity) 'I'm not going to let this thing get the better of me'. These people are the friends and neighbours that we have who seem never to allow themselves to be beaten by a cold or minor flu: they are often extroverts or organizers, and the majority are women. It is hard not to admire the courage of someone who, faced with a life-threatening diagnosis, responds with vigour and courage. 'I'll beat it, I keep busy so I don't have to think about it.' Janet's activity on the ward area caused immense frustration to the nurses but her 'therapy' to her fellow patients was more effective than any professional intervention.

The second adjustment style has been described as avoidance or denial. A typical example of this is a woman who, on introducing herself to a new staff nurse on surgical ward, commented on her condition by saying, 'They just cut off my breast as a precaution.' There seems to be, here, a refusal to enter into the seriousness or the reality of the diagnosis. While this may be an appropriate response during the stage of coming to terms with illness, it raises issues about patient autonomy and choice. How appropriate does the health care professional feel this particular coping mechanism to be? If a person chooses to get on with life without thinking about the cancer, or indeed by denying it, then how should those around them respond? When is it right to challenge this kind of denial or avoidance? How good is it for one's deeper health to deny important reality?

The third coping mechanism is described as fatalism. Michael demonstrates this as he refuses any help and resigns himself to his diagnosis. It is clear to the nurse that his assertion 'I am getting better' is not expressed with conviction but in the hope that it would keep the distance between the two. Michael sees (or chooses?) that he does not want to exert control over his diagnosis, and in that sense the consequences of this lack of control are accepted at this stage of his journey. Of course this passive acceptance can take both positive and negative forms. To the chaplain patients often say, rather negatively and passively: 'It's all in the hands of God.' More positively the patient might say, particularly if they are older: 'I've had a jolly good life, what's left is a bonus.'

The fourth coping mechanism is that of helplessness and hopelessness. Both Robert and Michael reflect the sense of being overwhelmed and engulfed by the sheer enormity of cancer. Looking the facts in the face, how could it be otherwise? There is a terror about the brutality of this disease that numbs almost all normal activity. Often the patient is unable to articulate his or her deep sense of existential pain and despair. The diagnosis is such an overwhelming threat and loss that it seems no control can be exerted over the situation. The inevitable negative outcome is experienced as if it had already come about. It is as if some patients say: 'There is nothing I can do to help myself.' Some die before they die as they retreat into their despair and pain.

Margaret is a fair reflection of the fifth and final survival schema which is that of anxious pre-occupation. Clearly for Margaret the diagnosis is a major threat and she struggles with her considerable uncertainty about the possibility of exerting control over the situation which gives rise to feelings of anxiety about the future. Some individuals cope by expressing a compulsive search for reassurance which reflects various forms of anxiety. A woman who had been re-admitted for some treatment after having had a diagnosis of cancer some ten years earlier said that she had worried every day for ten years that her cancer would come back, and at times she had mild panic attacks as she searched for the symptoms of its return. Some people may turn to complementary medicine for healing or demand of their religion and of God an intervention to take the cancer away. In Margaret's case, her anxious preoccupation takes the form of an excessive desire for understanding and information. The question, 'Why has this happened to me?' is a common one. It is often feared by many health care profession-als.

Part of the task of the pastor, confronted with this diversity of ways of reacting to illness, is to try and describe the world created by God as well as possible. We are answerable for the accuracy of our observations and our capacity to interpret what we see and what we experience. With this in mind, it is important to continue to emphasize the complex interconnec-tion between the physical and non-physical. That is to say, if health care professionals narrow the approach simply to the disease, the physical, then care will always be limited and limiting. This is where the concept of spiritual care is fundamental in the process of helping individuals and groups to explore the myths, meanings and re-evaluations around their coping mechanisms in illness.

There is then an important distinction to make between spiritual needs and religious needs. There is a spiritual dimension independent of various conceptual interpretations of it. The picture that best helps me to understand this is that of the Well and the Cathedral. The Well represents our common stock of feelings and thoughts about life's meaning and purpose. It is the collective sense of humankind's striving for an understanding of who we are, where we are going and what life means. Some may never choose to address this dimension of their life; many are forced to do so by crisis or illness.

The Cathedral, on the other hand, represents the contructions, whether of our own making or shaped by society, that we build or find, in order to help us address the questions, feelings and thoughts in the Well.

We may call this whole area, at the level of both Well and Cathedral, 'spiritual'. It takes many forms, some at first sight surprising, when it comes to the level of Cathedral, that is, some kind of construction wherein meaning is found and we are able to make some sense of ourselves. For some, even the department store or shopping centre may be the place that gives a sense of direction, purpose and hope. Others may look for their community (and so in a sense their anaesthetic) in the local public house. The escape of shared conversation over alcohol has long been an established habit within the community! Some find their sense of direction and purpose through sport, art or music; through a recreational pursuit; or simply within the framework of marriage and family. Others may, by choice or habit, find that some of these questions are addressed through faith, whether in Christianity or another religion. Here, what we have called 'the spiritual' finds perhaps its most explicit articulation – in 'the religious'.

As we survey these varied constructions, it is plain that spiritual needs are connected but far from the same for everybody. Many of the coping mechanisms discussed in this chapter are spiritual, that is, connected with the emotional responses of the kind we have called 'spiritual', regardless of their being given a 'God' or religious interpretation. Sometimes in the pastor's work the spiritual and the religious are very closely connected. In a Christian perspective, it is worth discussing what difference is made if a theological interpretation is given. Sometimes, spiritual and religious needs seem inextricably bound up together.

Spiritual pain is a term that is often used to describe a specific form of disease in the dying. Some thought has been given to it within the context of the hospice movement. All of the case studies above reflect living at a time of crisis with the Well, in spiritual pain. These are people who are trying to make sense of their experience – struggling to come to terms with their fears of the unknown, their anger, guilt or incomprehension. Within this context people often ask where God is in their pain. Sometimes they want to know if it is clear that their disease is terminal and what their dying will be like. Often there is curiosity about what exists beyond death. Some people simply feel pained at the lost opportunities in their life and want in some way to make amends, build new relationships, live life as fully as possible in the present, in their remaining time. What is clear to those involved in pastoral care is that this pain has a significant interconnecting effect on physical pain and can take many forms: anxiety, fear, breathlessness and so on. The voices of illness in this chapter challenge us to recognize non-physical symptoms of disease: to understand the spiritual as an integral part of a human being. Far too often teams of health care professionals fail to work together for the patient. Spiritual disease is not recognized: it is often ignored or simply left for others to sort out. Carers too may well have their own spiritual questions from deep within their own 'Wells', to be answered and dealt with.

In the encounter with illness how should the pastor respond? How much realism is desirable and right morally, in Christian or other terms? Prudence and Christian faith may point in different directions, but the issue needs airing and attending to with care and sensitivity. The voices can be heard in different ways. The process of human communication is complex and fraught with difficulty. One key aspect of the process of coping relates to the way in which the diagnosis is given, and in particular how information is shared. Many nurses have often had the experience of being present when the doctor shares some painful news with the patient, only to return later to realize that this information has been neither heard nor understood. This is understandably difficult. However, crucial to the person's recovery or to the nature of their death is the way in which they understand the personal meaning of (in this case) cancer. The person who shares the information has a crucial effect upon how that construction of meaning takes place for the individual in the context of their family or friends.

One of the feelings that undergirds voices here is the sense of a loss of control. People feel helpless as they experience treatment as something 'done for you'; many patients adapt quickly to a passive role. Within this process of adaptation there is often a search to make sense and to ask why. The questions and issues may be simple: a matter of understanding the treatment or knowing why they are taking particular forms of medication. If this search is undertaken unaided it may lead to confusion, misconceptions and fear. Knowledge is important because it gives confidence and control. The voices of illness, therefore, tell the health care professional to involve patients in decision making wherever possible. They ask that we think out what level of promotion of self-care is appropriate within the context of home or hospital. Too often autonomy is taken away from the patient.

The other emotion experienced has often been described as feeling as if one is 'riding on a roller-coaster'. Patients feel weepy, on edge, experience frustration, rage and annoyance which are all compounded by tiredness. Normal emotional controls become fragile and unreliable. The waiting and the delay in treatment, and unexpected events can be very traumatic. The end of treatment can, therefore, be viewed with mixed delight and fear. The journey back home can feel like a liberation and a new beginning for some, but for others the ward environment may be so secure and comforting that they have anxiety about going home, where there may be a lack of support and encouragement. These feelings within the voices of illness need reassurance and support. This can often take the practical form of good organization, where investigations and results are co-ordinated quickly so that patients are informed and their way forward is smoothed.

Another significant emotion underlying the voices, one that is often expressed non-verbally, is that of isolation. The person feels isolated because of weakness, perhaps an inability to write and the forgetfulness which impairs the ability of a patient to perform normal recreational pursuits. This isolation can always be reduced when there is an opportunity to talk, often quite informally. Within this experience, patients best support one another within a ward or out-patient area because they understand what each is going through.

Common to all responses to chronic illness are the emotional reactions of anxiety, anger, guilt, sadness and depression. The pastor needs to know what underlies each of the emotions expressed. All of us feel anxious when we are conscious of danger or vulnerability. All physical impairment, disfigurement or invalidity are sources of threat and danger that give rise to anxiety. The tendency is to offer reassurance too quickly. We must be ready to stay with the perfectly valid anxiety. There is nothing that can be said that takes away a mother's preoccupation with her children, or a man's concern that his hospitalization robs him of his nurturing role as the breadwinner for the family.

Individuals and communities will respond with anger when they suffer from a sense of unjustified attack. The personal domain of an individual is attacked by illness and therefore there may be questions about physical safety and self-esteem. This experience is an attack on the rules and values which a person holds very dear, as often there is a sense of the unjustness of a threat or of the effects of the threat on personal safety. Sometimes this finds expression by being focussed on the doctor or nurse. People will want to ask: 'Will the doctor be able to control the pain?' or 'Will they really look after me however bad it gets?' There is a sense here that an *agent*, either personal or impersonal, is abusing them. This anger might be expressed towards a spouse or the doctors or God. People might identify with other people's suffering or, indeed, project it out on to the organization or institution. Angry patients are often non-compliant patients who disrupt the normal routine of the ward or the GP's surgery. In part, they may be fighting to retain their dignity and autonomy as human agents.

Some research has suggested that patients who suppress anger and conform to the routine have a poor prognosis with malignant melanoma. It seems that within some cultures particular feelings are more socially acceptable than others; for example, sadness and fear may be acceptable but anger less so and more problematical. The voice of illness might not be expressed in calm measured tones but have the energy, power and freedom of a scream of anger, all the more so for being repressed or resisted.

It is interesting to note the amount of guilt that undergirds some of the voices in illness. It has, at its base, a sense of self-blame. In this process of apportioning blame, the guilty more often than not blame themselves. This is a very significant emotion in both people who have religious commitment and those who have none. Many believe that in some way, rationally or irrationally, the illness has happened as a result of some fault of their own making. Perhaps this is a natural result of people wanting to understand why – to build up a sense of meaning in their illness and to see that in moral terms. The question that they answer is: 'Am I being punished?' If they can find some way of expiating their sin, gaining control over it, then they might be able to overcome the guilt. Patients can often become fixated and it is not easy to help them move on. This takes the form: 'If only I hadn't done that, I might not have become ill.' This line of thought may arise irrespective of there being elements of reasonableness behind it.

The reaction of sadness and depression is, of course, about a sense of loss or defeat. This best takes expression in the voice of Robert. There is a sense of loneliness and isolation, of separation from all that was valued as important and real. Sometimes people can retreat into a world of loss and despair. There are people who find it impossible to articulate it and escape into sleep or silence.

There is then in the process of coming to terms with illness a re-evaluation of the myths about what the illness might mean.

The pastoral and theological dimension is significant here. It can seem, from this perspective, that it is not the objective consequences of disease but rather the ways in which they are interpreted that are of prime importance, and determine a person's health and wellbeing. These reactions are often shaped by a variety of factors that lead to a number of different myths and meanings. Above all, what is clear is that a person's adjustment can be fundamentally changed by the kind of support that they are given.

4

Stigma, Prejudice and Projections:

Exploring illness as a social and cultural reality

- **Josh**

I am a volunteer with my local AIDS support group, working on the telephone information line and attend a weekly support group for people living with HIV disease. I have been involved in all this for the past three years and it has become very much part of my life; many of the people I meet have become my friends.

After one support group, we had just finished the meeting and I offered to help with the washing up. As I looked out of the window over the local video shop I found myself drying the mug with extra care and vigour. I took the tea-towel and rubbed the inside of the mug with enormous care. I felt a strange level of fear and anxiety. In the pub afterwards I was both surprised and shocked that my anxiety had come out so strongly in my behaviour with the mug. The rigour with which I found myself wiping away the moisture from the mug related to my fear of the possiblity of catching the virus from these dirty cups. Despite my awareness training and my long attachment with this issue this level of fear and anxiety surprised me.

- **St Gabriel's Parochial Church Council**

I have been asked to attend a meeting of a Church Council to enable them to address the subjects of AIDS and HIV. Before the meeting the rector celebrates the eucharist and I notice that all twenty-three members of the group choose not to take the chalice but to communicate by dipping the host into the chalice, thereby avoiding any contact with it. I find this curious but also sense, intuitively, that something is wrong.

At the meeting I begin to focus the task of the group by attempting to underline the reality that AIDS and HIV is an issue for us all. Three very articulate members of the group stand up and, in turn, challenge my assumption that AIDS has anything to do with them. These three speakers have widespread agreement within the group. I ask the group why they all individually chose to have no contact with the chalice. There is silence followed quickly by anger. I am told by one member of the group that how they choose to receive communion is none of my business and by another that Holy Communion has nothing to do with AIDS or HIV. When I ask, 'Could this act have anything to do with your fear of contagion?' the response is overwhelming and aggressive. Half of the PCC members get up and walk out and the rector is forced to close this particular part of the meeting and go on to the next piece of business.

● **Patricia**

I am a 36 year-old living in a half-way house, having been discharged from the local mental hospital two years ago. I've been resident in the hospital for over ten years with a long history of depression and acute mental illness. Life is hard and I find it really difficult to cope with. I realize that I don't fit in; I smoke very heavily and can't concentrate on things for very long. I feel insecure and unhappy most of the time. People look at me in a funny way and I know that mothers grab their children closer when I go into the local Macdonalds for some food. I felt safe in the hospital and cared for. The staff understood and I felt a part of the place. Life is hard and the world unsafe. I have my own room but I don't feel part of this place – I would go back to my hospital but they have closed it.

● **Alison**

I am a middle-aged professional woman coping (I think) with

severe disability as a result of a car accident three years ago. It has taken a long time to get to some kind of mobility and I returned to work after a long period of rehabilitation. I have to live with a considerable amount of pain, discomfort and the struggle to live as normally as possible. Disability is not something you accept – it is a constant struggle. Yes, of course, it is a struggle that goes on inside me. A struggle with my self-image; anxiety about the future and the dialogue between my need for independence and inevitable assent to the dependence that comes with my failing body!

However, the struggle is also with the world – external attitudes that disable me and deepen my pain. There is the obvious physical struggle – the world looks very different in a wheelchair – imagine it in your mind. There are, however, the assumptions most of us have about health, normal existence, and stability. People's attitudes disable me. Most mean well, though I want, if at all possible, to have autonomy and independence. I don't want crushing kindness and people to take over stuff for me. I need empowering help to live with the loss and the paradoxes. I hate the easy reassurances, the 'Just think of others worse off than yourself' routine! I don't find it easy asking for or receiving help.

• Anthony

I am a 26 year-old man living in a residential home for severely disabled people. I'm as normal as you can get inside myself; above average intelligence; an interest in literature and art. However, my body is bloody useless. I need help with all functions of living: dressing, toilet, eating and moving.

These homes are curious places. They are full of kindness, compassion, support and love. Some of the residents give in to it. They want to be cared for, supported and loved. Some of the carers get into all this for all kinds of reasons and I wish some of them would try and understand why. It might make them better carers! What I find most difficult is the individualism and protectionism of the place. The majority of the residents want this kind of protection. I don't if it's protection for its own sake and if it doesn't involve me. I want a voice and I demand that my voice is listened to.

The other great area of my interest is the political world. I want to do everything that I possibly can to effect change: better human rights for disabled people. This is about changing attitudes and society to make it a better place for disabled people. That involves me in all kinds of action – some of which should make people feel uncomfortable and challenged. How else will life change and grow? How else will I play my part in that movement?

• Margaret

I have just come back from my local church study group which is discussing the Anglican bishops' report on sexuality. I am a lesbian woman with a daughter. I work as a journalist on the local newspaper. My local vicar is very supportive and understanding and very much wanted me to share my story with the group. He felt that it would be best for the group to respond to the 'reality' rather than some words on paper.

I wish I hadn't done it. A couple didn't seem much bothered but the rest were shocked and inflicted their fears and prejudices on me. One lady felt concerned about my daughter: 'Children need a stable man and woman' (how many of them are there about?); and others didn't feel it was normal. One older man even asked me whether I'd had any treatment as if I was suffering from some terrible illness. I wonder whether it was all worth it?

• David

I have been living with the virus for four years now. The AIDS Unit in my local hospital have been great in giving me appropriate support and information. Perhaps I shouldn't have been as open, but I really wanted to tell people and let them know how things were for me, so they could support me when the going got bad. It was hell. I stopped going to church because of the uproar it all caused. The vicar refused to speak to me and told me that I should keep it all to myself. Work colleagues were horrified and a group even tried to get me removed. The difficulties have eased now but two were so angry and upset they applied for and were granted a transfer to another office. I will never forget what some people said to me. What a terrible thing fear is.

★

In some respects, the encounter with illness through the stories in this book demonstrates that the real disaster or tragedy of illness is not just the nature of the disease, but often the processes by which illness is perceived. This point is exemplified by listening to those individuals and communities most affected by HIV disease. It follows that it might be argued that the disaster of AIDS is one of perception. From this it would follow that part of the practical challenge of responding to illness is to enable people to perceive the reality of how and why illness is described in the way that it is. The response to illness is bound to be a complex mixture of feelings and emotions. Josh and David indicate something of their fear in response to their illness and Margaret experiences the reality of prejudice. Anthony thinks about the way in which his society organizes its response to disabled people and Alison bears testimony to the reality that the disabling factor in her struggle focusses upon attitudes just as much as the physical condition. This demonstrates that diseases have social, ethical and political dimensions. Illnesses affect individuals and groups, not abstract entities or collectives, and affect them in a variety of ways according to their social condition and degree of bodily health.

Individuals and groups also use their illness in a variety of ways. Those groups most affected by HIV disease have used the disease to argue for equal rights, for greater justice and action against discrimination and prejudice. This is provoked by the way in which meaning is attached to illness. Take the example of St Gabriel's Parochial Church Council. Their reaction reflects a particular understanding of contagion, both physical and moral, in relation to the virus. They bear testimony to the truth that HIV and AIDS have become symbolic bearers of a range of anxieties about our contemporary culture. For some AIDS is symbolic of a society that has lost its way; where the social composition of communities is fragmented, involving fundamental challenges to racial boundaries, social marginality and, above all, confusion about moral configurations. How are we to draw the boundary between what is right and what is wrong? How are we to relate to those people and groups who are different from us? Disability, mental illness and aspects of sexuality reflect upon the way in which we invest illness with particular meaning and project a number of our anxieties and fears on to it. Related to this there is a need for groups to look for a scapegoat of some sort, to be expelled from society. Thus many mental hospitals were built on the outskirts of towns and cities. In recent years, health education has had to face the challenge of persuading the general population that AIDS is everybody's issue rather than a particular group's problem. It is comparable to the way that witches in seventeenth-century England were widely used as scapegoats for all kinds of beliefs, anxieties and fears.

It may be interesting to explore whether Christians respond to perceptions of illness in a different way from others. In what way might the Christian tradition have something distinctive to offer in the area of exploration into illness? Simon Garfield, in his book *The End of Innocence*, maps out a history of the responses to AIDS over the past decade. Garfield allows a number of individuals and representatives of groups and organizations to tell their story of response to AIDS. He gives a picture of political intrigue; panic, hysteria and prejudice; wasted opportunities and financial mismanagement; and a medical and scientific battle conducted against what seemed impossible odds. The church's involvement in this is part of the wider picture: a mixture of quite extraordinary courage and achievement interwoven with a fantastic tale of struggle against prejudice, panic, professional rivalry, political in-fighting and incompetent crisis management. Some particular Christian responses have been compassionate and life-giving, while others have been prejudiced, death-dealing, ignorant and damnable.

There is one key thread in this particular tapestry that deserves further exploration. This concerns the search for meaning in illness. The meaning may be social, psychological, spiritual, medical or personal. The search is necessary if perceptions are to be valid and appropriate. Doctors need to find the medical meaning of the symptoms of a disease in order to prescribe a particular form of treatment. All those struggling with illness ask questions at some stage about what it means in their own personal context. Some may find support through psychotherapy, enabling them to make connections between their present distress or unease and formative experiences that shape emotional and personal habits and life styles. Others may look to spirituality or theology to explain or to give purpose and depth to the experience of illness. When those people respond to Alison, 'just think of others worse off than yourself', they impose a kind of meaning on to the disability that attempts to reassure. When Margaret, confronted with the concern about her daughter in the statement 'children need a stable man and woman', she is faced with moral assumptions about the nature of parenthood and family, as if there were a single meaningful framework within which children should be brought up and a sharp distinction in meaning between the normal and the abnormal. Within this exploration there may be a helpful distinction to be made between appropriate and inappropriate meaning. Whilst respecting that individuals may find strength and meaning by a whole variety of means, what is interesting in relation to HIV and AIDS is whether some moral meaning is better than none. There is some suggestion in a variety of writings that the virus entered into some kind of moral vacuum in order to teach humankind lessons about our behaviour and interaction.

The challenge to understand what illness means from a variety of perspectives is a constant theme throughout this book. How are we to understand illness? Is it an accident of nature or act of God? For some, in relation to AIDS, and these might be represented by St Gabriel's Parochial Church

Council, illness has a clear meaning: it is an indication of God's punishment on individuals for their wickedness. Which meaning is better: that AIDS is a fault in creation or that it is a deliberate punishment of God? Some theological writers seek to emphasize the distinction between reasons for an illness (physical, social etc.) and the meaning of the experience of the illness. In this respect AIDS is not special. This distinction could be applied to many other cases (for example lung cancer and smoking). As far as meaning goes, we ought to say that we are being brought to a *peirasmos*, a test which focusses our response to God. While this approach is attractive, what does it say to the person living with AIDS, or, indeed, about the way in which God reveals meaning and truth in our lives? If God is in the AIDS crisis bringing us to the test, where is God in the cancer, the mental illness or the sudden accident causing disability? Are such evils satisfactorily explicable along these lines? This aspect of the subject is fundamental for it asks about the way in which God reveals meaning and truth in our lives. God may be revealed through the transformation we experience in this process but what picture does it give us of the nature of God? Is it not a strange route to a good end? One might say that God does not directly cause the illness – it comes from the 'system' which he 'lets be': the idea of test can still be a suitable reading for us to make. There are many people who believe in God while no longer seeing him as crudely acting in the details of the system.

There are situations where there is a plausible moral element in illness. People who drive under the influence of drink cause accidents. People who smoke run a very high risk of developing cancer. Within the conversation about meaning there must be a balance to be achieved through holding together an approach which offers a non-judgmental acceptance on the one hand, and an awareness of the individual's power for good or ill on the other.

The stories described above do give some indication of what kind of pastoral response might be appropriate in the face of illness as a cultural and social reality. David, Margaret, Anthony and Alison speak of the need for an unconditional acceptance and a quality of engagement and listening that may communicate their value as individuals created in the image of God, no matter what their condition, their behaviour and feelings. This might be described as an *acceptance ethic*, whereby individuals can begin to free themselves from externally imposed judgments and find the 'locus of evaluation' within themselves, but derived ultimately from God's valuing of them. This can happen in a community or residential home where the dignity, independence and voice of those with mental or physical disability are respected, listened to and acted upon. This response starts with the recognition of the dignity of each person: the only positive standard by which individuals should be judged is their awareness of their own being in all its complexity. To use theological language, this is the principle of how unconditional love can set people free from the dead letter of the law (be it medical, psychological or theological dogma) and fill and empower them with a new spirit of freedom and peace.

There is a long history of diseases having a range of metaphors and meanings attached to them. For many years both cancer and tuberculosis expressed in contemporary culture a number of ideas about energy and feeling, strength and weakness that derive from a concern about the place of these attributes within the social order. Illness was frightening because it reflected a breakdown within the accepted understanding and economy of life. For example, the response to consumption saw the body as like a mismanaged economy that wastes away when its energy is spent recklessly or when desire is not checked. In imagery relating to cancer, and to an extent AIDS, we find unregulated growth and a repressed desire: the body is 'hijacked' by 'subversive' cells with a life of their own, often, it is popularly thought, as a result of the repression of feeling and energy or the loss of morale. This idea finds expression in many self-help books that encourage their readers to a positive attitude over the illness in question and may, in some respects, arise once more out of the search for some kind of causal meaning: where did the virus come from, and why me rather than anybody else?

Sometimes diseases can be used as metaphors for what is feared and people may even find themselves involved in caring as a way of coping with their own fears about illness and death, as in Anthony's story. In the popular imagination, ideas of decay, pollution and weakness become attached to diseases whose causality is murky and for which treatment is ineffectual. So AIDS stands in a historical tradition of leprosy and syphilis as well as cancer, all of them associated with decay, pollution and disorder. All these illnesses have been used as metaphors to enliven charges that our society is corrupt or unjust, by individuals or groups who wish to exert some kind of control and impose order within the framework of social meaning. The desire by Margaret's local church to be highly prescriptive in its definition of parenthood is related to an understandable desire to see a structure of meaning through social order. The reality that traditional patterns of family life are changing or, as some would argue, breaking down, along with the emergence of HIV disease, gives many an opportunity to give voice to their fears about the relationship of social disorder to sexual irregularity. This relates to the perceived fragmentation and rapid change of society and culture towards the end of the twentieth century. If only society could be made more orderly, a framework of meaning agreed and imposed, the health of the population would improve.

These aspects of thought and response touch on the roots of sexual anxiety in particular, which is ultimately seated in the human body itself and in attitudes to the personal self and body images. In her book, *Natural Symbols*, the social anthropologist Mary Douglas argues that a group or society expresses itself by what it does to the human body. The physical body is a kind of map of the social body. Taboos surrounding the surface of the physical body – and especially the orifices of the body – symbolize points of anxiety about the boundaries of the social body. Typically, it follows that the society concerned about having a clear identity and well-defined boundaries will symbolize this concern in the attempt to exert a high degree of control of its members' physical bodies.

Seen in this light, AIDS raises crucial questions about what the boundaries of our life are and what the limits of tolerance ought to be. In other words, questions of identity and control of the human body bear heavily on the understanding of representations of HIV infection and our response to it. AIDS has challenged and questioned the meanings, values and practices in which the experiences of sexuality, love, the body, life, death and physical processes are grounded. Put another way, illness is constructed through language and, in particular, through the discourses of medicine and science. But this construction is 'true and real' only in specific ways, for example, in so far as it successfully guides research or facilitates control over illness. Meanwhile, other discourses construct illness in quite different ways, that seem harder to authenticate or pin down but are exceedingly powerful. Perhaps a new approach to illness is required that can hold together this whole range of meanings and responses. It is inevitable that there will always be a number of meanings around illness, and therefore our encounter with it should take us beyond the medical and scientific into the social, political and ethical areas where meanings also are formed. In some ways, as the disabled people argue above, the social dimension can be more significant, more persuasive and central than the medical and scientific. No one framework can sum up the truth of illness; science or indeed theology is no longer the only base which generates meaning and reality. The processes by which our images of the social realities of illness are shaped and formed are fundamental to the encounter. The context within which we meet our illness shapes the experience and our perceptions of what is happening to us. Perhaps we need to explore new images of disease and ask how these conceptions and constructions relate to our own individual sense of security or insecurity about the meaning of life and how far we can exercise any control over it. Is it possible to deliver the Western image of disease from the fear of collapse and the sense of dissolution which can and does contaminate our encounter?

Human fears and anxieties are handled in a variety of ways. Sometimes the fear of collapse and the anxiety about illness that relates to identity are projected on to the world as a way of coping with it. There can be a sharp division between strength and weakness, the well and the sick, as the anxiety and fear are handled within the encounter with illness, in order to localize it, contain it and domesticate it. It is others that become ill: we can be protected from any danger of contamination through a sharp drawing of boundaries and by fixing a distance that protects us, the healthy, so we keep our anxieties at bay.

It follows then that within the social forces at work, certain models of disease are used as means of social control. Theology has played its part in the shaping and formation of some of these models in its desire for God-given order and structure and in the drawing out of a framework of systematic thought. There is a kind of splitting mechanism that goes on here in the process of doing theology, whereby in order to maintain control and construct secure frameworks, individuals and groups distance the sense of uncertainty, chaos, darkness and fear. In this context, categories of difference are constructed; for example, we construct the idea of the patient in a strongly distinctive sense, ensuring clear boundaries between the healthy observer, doctor or lay person and the patient. Anthony gives voice to how this particular dimension of meaning finds its voice and shape through the way some residential homes are organized for disabled people, with carers and patients aware of the demarcation between them. This boundary making ultimately denies the realization that Josh struggles with as he dries his mug, the reality that we are all at risk in the sense that we will all be ill at some stage in our lives, will fail and will ultimately die. It comes out theologically in the tension between God as the powerful creator and orderer and God as the vulnerable saviour who is alongside us on the cross. We need to resist forcing God into our own dichotomies. For the Christian the God of the cross is one with the Creator.

Among the many ways in which illness has been represented, stigma is amongst the most significant. AIDS, like mental disability, has for many years been set out in terms of intense devaluation, dishonour and degradation. AIDS is connected to stigmatized groups, it is sexually transmitted and it is terminal. This is where and why language is so important.

Any reconstruction of the framework for understanding illness must take into consideration the power of fear in the human psyche. Further, as AIDS specifically continues to be a source of panic and threat to health and community, feelings are sometimes intensified by the growing awareness of the fallibility of medicine. For many social theorists, death has become the omnipresent symbol of our time; and to the images of Auschwitz, Hiroshima and Vietnam, AIDS may surely be added. These theorists, however, often overstate the symbolic power of death, since most cultures in the past have had to live with the effect of plague, pestilence, poverty, famine and early death (and indeed, still do today in the non-Western world), all on scales far greater than death so far induced by AIDS.

The voices of the contributions with which we began give some indication of the kind of engagement that is needed in the light of the encounter with HIV disease and mental and physical disability as a result of which people have to face social stigmatization. All this says much about the kind of culture we live in and how we grow up in our understanding and education. The encounters with these people induce in us a confidence in their reasonableness and co-operativeness. Therefore the strategy for helping must attribute any evidence of selfishness to the destructive effects of an inhumane society which has failed to teach people basic life-skills and perceptions. The difficulties of the encounters, in other words, say more about the world in which we live and the way in which it teaches us to be human than about the true character of illness. The Christian tradition believes that every person has the power to be selfish or destructive (that is, to sin) and, therefore, each person needs to have an awareness of sin for the sake of understanding his or her own need for wholeness. Non-judgmental acceptance and the assumption that we can inhabit a morally neutral world is not enough for wholeness. The theological basis of this response rejects the locking of each person into the prison of his or her own individuality, and encourages each of us to believe that openness, flexibility and self-acceptance will of themselves help to bring wisdom and fulfilment and are ways by which human beings can respond to the divine initiative of grace.

This response, crucially, excludes the finality of the tragic dimension from human existence. It holds that a sense of wrong (even if at times inappropriate) may also reveal aspects of human failure persons cannot remedy on their own. Guilt is transcended by that sense which in human experience points beyond our fallible moral values to a basic state of lostness and alienation which itself evokes grace.

This is why morality and spirituality cannot, in the end, be separated. It is why the encounter with the meanings of illness is so complex and challenging. It is impossible to be re-ductionist about the meaning of illness. The pastor's task, in part, is to enable individuals and groups to look at the representations of illness and what lies behind them. We need to know how language shapes reality for us and to be sensitive about words and how they are used. Above all, within this discourse the voices of those most affected by illness need to be listened to so that new ways of thinking might emerge and develop. This positive creative task of the mending and re-minting of discourse should be the focus of pastoral theology. For illness is ultimately, and most importantly, about people. In the midst of pastoral reflection is the human reality of people who are struggling with disease. The pastoral conversation, as a mode of discourse that exists around illness, should make possible an understanding of what it means to those affected by it; that is, to all of us. There is a continued need for public education not only to convey the facts about illness but also to embody a response to it which can discover appropriate meaning in the moral complexity. The complexity is that of a world in which, amid prejudice and false imaging, the dead are mourned, the sick and dying cared for, sensible precautions against infection adopted, and life and sexuality enjoyed, not desperately but steadily. The hermeneutical task is to deepen human solidarity through pastoral conversation; conversation that appreciates the power of words and discourse and how representations in language affect pastoral practice.

5

Separation, Alienation and Powerlessness:

Exploring experiences of pastoral care

- ## Howard

  I lie in bed conscious of the noise and activity of the busy ward.
  It has been nine days since the ambulance brought me in – I feel
  disorientated; my body aches; I can't concentrate and wish that
  I could feel more myself. The doctors don't understand what is
  wrong with me – they continue to ask questions, take blood and
  use me for their medical students. I am worried and I wonder
  what on earth will happen to this useless body that isn't
  responding to any positive thinking on my part! They are kind
  to me on the ward. The sister explains the procedures and the
  domestic always picks out the dead flowers from my vase and
  asks how I am. All this human contact and kindness reinforces
  my separation, my pain and powerlessness.

- ## Robert

  Robert is a young energetic theological student training for
  ministry in a large college. Unexpectedly he is taken ill and
  ordered by the doctor to rest his spine with bed rest. During the
  next four weeks he is subjected to an endless succession of visits
  from his fellow students. With several exceptions, he finds the
  majority of his 'caring' colleagues further paralysing. He is
  surprised at their superficial contact, and their inability to listen
  to his feelings. He feels shocked by their self-absorption and the
  distance between his bed-bound body and their chatter. Above
  all, he is disturbed by the transparency of their motivations to
  come and be kind to him. He wonders about his, and their
  vocation to care. What needs are being fulfilled for professional

religious carers? Would his approach have been any different in similar circumstances? Pastoral care should have a church health warning attached to it!

- ## Josephine

Josephine is a middle-aged GP in hospital for routine surgery. She is sitting out in her chair the afternoon before the operation reading *The Guardian* newspaper. From the corner of her eye she sees and hears a chaplain at the far end of the ward. She's intrigued by this and tries not to be obvious in paying attention to how the chaplain goes about her work. She gets the impression that the chaplain is intruding, albeit rather nicely, into the ward's life. She hears the chaplain two beds away say, 'Good afternoon dear, I'm the chaplain, now tell me what's up with you.' Josephine is horrified – what a patronizing intrusion into that person's life; and then is further surprised when the patient spills out all of his worries and troubles to the chaplain who seems to listen carefully and sympathetically. She thinks to herself, 'I can't be doing with this', and buries her head into the newspaper. She has not spoken to a clergy person in years – what on earth are they doing in a hospital? She feels torn: part of her would like to talk out of curiosity and part of her feels that she wants no interruptions or intrusions. She hears the chaplain's bleep go and watches her leave the ward with mixed feelings of relief and disappointment.

- ## Sara

Sara is back at home now after a long period in hospital during which she underwent major treatment for cancer. She has recently had two bereavements: her mother and her husband – which have been devastating experiences. During her period of hospitalization it was suggested that she should see a counsellor to help her through these two rapid bereavement experiences. While she can't remember in precise detail the shape and content of the conversation with the counsellor, the memory of that encounter is still painful. She talks about how the counsellor interpreted her feelings, described them as being 'like a frightened little girl', and made all kinds of interpretations about her family and the cause of her pain and woundedness. She felt that the encounter was coercive and destructive. While she is sure that some of her difficulties may emerge from experiences in her family, she felt the counsellor made too many assumptions and moved too quickly into this precious and intimate part of her life.

• Leslie

The slow recovery at home was broken by my second near-death experience, this time with a pulmonary embolism. Now I've spent two weeks in a Cheshire hospital – amenities semi-modern, but care of the highest quality. Of all my spells in hospital, this was the one when my sensibilities were most acute: emotionally I was susceptible to every kindness and gesture of support – which I received in plenty. It was as if I were going through a tear-jerking movie. Perhaps the illness was especially debilitating, but the effect was that this time I was particularly ready to receive every care and help the hospital could provide. And every aspect of hospital life that was relevant to my condition provided its share: daily nursing; physiotherapy; medical supervision.

Oddly and mysteriously to me as a religious person is the effect of the one notable omission in the experience of hospital care. At no point in my periods in hospital have I had any significant encounter with the ministry of chaplains. Perhaps I have never been there quite long enough ('He generally comes on a Friday' – though not it appears that Friday); and I have never felt moved to activate priestly attentions. I wonder why this is. By temperament I do not like to make a fuss or seek special treatment. But there is more than that. Somehow hospital life, the enclosed world of the bed and the ward, seems all-sufficient. Let its sequence of events take its course – no need for intrusions from outside except when visitors appear, and even they seem sometimes like strangers not belonging in what so rapidly becomes our world, where only patients and staff have any right to be. It is very intense while it lasts, through quickly put aside – and without regrets – when the day of release comes. Perhaps I am easily institutionalized. At all events, even God did not seem to me compellingly necessary to this little, busy world.

As one whose ordinary life has a good deal of scope for initiative, I am surprised how easily hospital brings me to a state of passivity and aceptance. It goes further than just not wanting to cause a fuss, though that tendency is certainly part of it. It may be partly a readiness to resign myself to be cared for, a relapse into some of the features of infancy. Not very macho anyway, hospital makes me into its direct opposite.

*

There is an inevitable distance between those who are living with illness and disability and others who look on, intervene in different ways and are charged to care. It is a mistake to believe that all pastoral care, by its very nature, is good or positive; indeed, as our case studies show the opposite can often be the case. For some, like Leslie, it is unnecessary, unwanted and irrelevant to the particular world which he inhabits. There is a loneliness about Howard's situation which human contact and kindness reinforce, and for Josephine and Sara the intervention of those who are carers is very questionable indeed. It may be that these interventions are not only questionable but inappropriate and dangerous.

These issues are related in part to ongoing debate about the meaning and practice of care. There is a long tradition within the Christian church of pastoral care exercised by representative Christian people in a variety of contexts to a range of individuals and groups. With the development of the human sciences has come an increased interest in the theory and practice of psychological care through psychotherapy and counselling. While some of the roots of this approach to human beings have links with the churches, many of the insights of counselling and psychotherapy belong to contrasting and conflicting ideologies. There have been many in the Christian churches who have taken up counselling, which has brought hope and healing to many. However, this enthusiasm for counsellinghas led, in many instances, to an uncritical adoption of secular and humanistic theories and methods, which under-value and stand over against aspects of traditional Christian pastoral ministry.

There is an issue here of how Christians in these roles might be empowered to use their theological resources in their work. Are there particular or distinctive values and beliefs which can support individuals and groups in their thinking and practice?

This is a particular issue for Christians who work in secular organizations. For a focus to explore these points let us take the situation of the health care chaplain working within the culture of the Health Service in the mid-1990s. Chaplains have experienced extraordinary levels of change in their professional and organizational lives as a result of the reform of the National Health Service in 1990. The future of chaplaincy as funded by hospitals and trusts is curiously insecure. As the shape of the reforms begins to establish and give structure to a radically new culture of health care organization and delivery, chaplains have been forced to ask far-reaching questions about their service and accountability. As the Health Service continues to undergo a process of decentralization, it will become increasingly difficult for chaplains to guard against the power of individual hospitals to choose how they want to spend their resources. Put crudely, a manager may decide that they will achieve a better service by employing a counsellor than a chaplain. Some chaplains may decide that their future security depends upon training in psychotherapy or counselling. My observation, as an active participant in all these changes, and as one who listens to professional colleagues, is that chaplains have not been empow-ered to use their theological resources for their work within this emerging culture.

Part of our inability to use theology may lie in theological training both of clergy and of lay people. If the theory of theology is difficult to put into practice and relate to experience, then there is an urgent need to explore how theology is taught and what models of doing theology are promoted in training. In part, this is understandable; it is a complex task. The theological scene and training are dominated by the quest for abstract truth and by historical enquiry (the Bible, doctrine etc.); they are often weak on hermeneutics of the kind that facilitates application in the pastoral sphere. The tendency to platitudes or simplistic ways of using biblical texts is evident in many aspects of our life and work. Some think that these are adequate and decline challenges to that adequacy, however obvious they may seem to others.

The question within the experience of pastoral care is: Does theology help us to engage with individuals and groups in order to understand the realities of their lives? Action might be preferred to thinking as providing more effective results for the chaplain's work; but uncritical or unreflective action may be dangerous and unhelpful. Pastoral theology may be more appropriately described as rooted in doing the job (as liberation theology focusses on praxis), and the task of exploring roles, models and meanings as an unaffordable luxury that does not produce results. Put another way, does theology change the way we act, think and work?

Part of the problem about understanding the meaning of pastoral care and about these searching questions concerning the nature of theology may lie in the understanding of truth. The language of theology often seems private and obscure, lacking publicly accessible significance. Hospitals are secular cultures with little or no sympathy for religion and its language. Their predominant values, philosophies and languages are held and promoted by managers in power. Within that culture perhaps the language of psychotherapy is a better ideology, a more effective truth? Will it support and facilitate better care? May it even be a bridge between the chaplain's language and that of the powerful managers?

In recent years there have been some significant critiques of therapy, not least by Jeffrey Masson. In his book *Against Therapy* he argues that all psychotherapy displays a lack of interest in social justice and an implicit acceptance of the political status quo. He holds that therapy, perhaps like theology, shows a certain lack of interest in the world. Most significant is the criticism that too many therapists fit what they experience into a highly structured ideology that informs them about human behaviour and relationships. There is then a kind of manipulation as therapists attempt to impose their own structures on their patients. There is even a question of experience being distorted to fit in with what the therapist believes to be true. Masson argues that the truth of a person's life cannot be uncovered by therapy and it is a fundamental myth that all therapy helps, regardless of the theoretical orientation of that therapy.

Others have highlighted the myth of training. While there has been an increased attempt to regularize therapeutic training within a system of accreditation, the reality is that often training is very modest and lacks any unified coherence. It is still the case that anyone can set themselves up as a therapist without safeguards or guidelines. This is changing and is bound to change further, but there are questions about the nature of professionalism and how far therapy is undergoing a process of self-critical evaluation of its values. Is therapy good pastoral care in so far as it attempts to change the world or is it to be merely an expression of the dominant view of society? Put another way, perhaps often the environment, the culture and the context need changing and not the individual. There are also important questions about the needs that are being fulfilled for the therapist in this type of work. Is the life of the therapist in any better shape than those of the patients? If we all have in common the same problems, fears and emotional insecurities, would the advice offered in the context of the therapeutic relationship be any better than that of a well-informed friend?

Perhaps the lesson to be learnt is that we need always to be reflective about the fixed ideology that turns people into experts. Aspects of the encounter with illness here warn against an over-identification with a narrow medical model. We need to offer the people we encounter choice, informality, a certain blurring of boundaries. The danger of therapy and some forms of pastoral care is that it is over-identified with medical education. Medical education is an education in problem solving: it takes an amorphous situation; structures it into a problem; and solves the problem. This is clear, black-and-white thinking, rational and down-to earth. The experience of illness does not easily fit into this ideology or framework.

These questions are ultimately questions of power. Any professional carer can use power to manipulate, control and humiliate. Sometimes this is unconscious and sometimes deliberate, but it is related to the issues of the knowledge base of the carer. Is the carer superior and the patient inferior? In some senses the professional carer, by virtue of his or her knowledge, training, experience and special insights, can work and think with a sense of some access to truth above and beyond the capacity of the people they encounter. The carer interprets the patient's truths and tells them what they 'really' mean. How authentic is this? Does it make for health or perhaps merely for an exercise of power? Power involves the right to have your definition of reality prevail over other people's definition, and in our society police, prisons, laws, the church and theology may be seen as tools by which one definition of reality or another can be made to prevail over others. Among the most dangerous people in the world are those who believe they know what is best for others. Sensitive pastoral care needs to be critical of such an approach, and the criticism must start with the carer. For carers can only suggest they know what is best for others when they themselves have failed to become aware that, being fallible human beings, they are likely to misinterpret reality and to mistake motives; and they are perhaps inclined to impute more noble motives to themselves than is actually the case. We see in illness the fragility and vulnerability of people. In any of the situations described above, it must always be true that those who have the power to save or help us also have the power to harm us. Of course some therapy works, but no therapy works perfectly.

This is most convincingly put by David Smail, who proposes an alternative to therapy in his book *Taking Care*. He argues that we suffer pain in the very process of therapy because we do damage to each other and we shall continue to suffer pain as long as that damage continues. It follows that the way to alleviate and mitigate distress is for us to 'take care of' the world

and the other people in it and not to 'treat' them. He believes
that most of the evils of our society are more or less directly
attributable to the unequal distribution of forms of economic
power which are abused and corrupting. This power should be
used to increase the power of those who lack it, to take care
rather than to treat, to enlighten rather than to mystify, to love
rather than to exploit, and in general to think seriously about
the obligations as opposed to the advantages of power. Smail
argues for a change of heart which is the rejection of that sense
of intrinsic badness and unacceptability which was instilled in
us when, as children, we were in the power of our parents and
teachers. There is then choice, and we need some kind of
context within which we can value and accept all that we are in
its complexity. There is a choice about value, which can change
our lives and our world if we choose to co-operate and share:
because if we value ourselves, we value others, now and to
come, and the planet in which we all live. This is a rejection of
those who seek to dominate and manipulate us.

It might be worth asking how this theory would affect the
stories of those shared in this book. For example, would Leslie
be best left without any explicit therapy which would burden
him with the emotional strain of it? This is an issue of power and
choice. People who are ill are not best placed to have their
'whole can of worms' opened up unless they choose to! The old
almoner stuck to practical therapy ('who'll see to you when you
go home?'): is that the best way, in sickness?

For some chaplains the acquisition of the skills of psychotherapy bestows a kind of security in the health-care
organization. To sell out to this particular model does not do
justice to the special and distinctive contribution that they can
make. The movement and dialogue between models and
approaches is complex. Would Christian theology (*true agape*)
release us from manipulation? Our historical record is not good:
but suppose one had and fought for a theology of freedom for
the individual as the image of God? Then, perhaps the
manipulative use of power and ideology might be kept in its
place.

6

Decisions, Dilemmas and Choices:
Exploring patient autonomy, ethics and options in illness

- **Sarah**

  Sarah is the mother of a 4 year-old boy suffering from cancer who wants him to be allowed to die without further painful medical intervention. Some of the doctors want to obtain a court order to seek the appointment of a legal guardian (*parens patrine*) in order that the muscle tumour can be treated with some thirty radiotherapy sessions each under a general anaesthetic – at the end of which there is a 30% chance of surviving. Other doctors on the case are opposed to any such treatment. The child does not seem to be adapting to treatments so far. The mother says that she, and not the doctors, will have to live with the consequences of the decision – and the same goes for any after-effects of the treatment, or indeed its failure.

- **Matthew**

  Matt is a 22 year-old student who has been injured in a road accident. It is now five months since his injury and he is in the condition called 'Persistent Vegetative State' (PVS). He swallows, breathes, absorbs nutrients from his gut, blinks and sometimes his eyes open and move around in his head without direction or focus. He is being kept alive by a nasogastive tube and occasional courses of antibiotics for chest infections. There are no electrical or clinical signs of activity in his cerebral cortex.

- **Roger**

Roger suffered severe head injuries in a fight outside his local pub in south London. He was admitted to the local Accident and Emergency Department and the doctors there decided he needed some specialized neurosurgical work. After failing to get an intensive care bed in London he was flown to a hospital in Nottingham by the RAF, where he later died.

- **Doreen**

Doreen is a 46 year-old single woman and has cancer of the breast. Her consultant wants to prescribe an aggressive course of chemotherapy to cure her. Doreen's nurse in the hospital thinks that she is unaware of the prognosis and that the side-effects are disproportionate to the outcome. There is a conflict between the doctor and the nurse at the present moment and Doreen is not involved in the process of making decisions and choices.

- **Stephen**

Stephen is a 46 year-old man who had a serious car accident in Hereford. He was flown by helicopter to the Regional Trauma Unit and transferred to the Intensive Therapy Unit two days later when his condition had stabilized. He continued in the intensive care bed for a period of fifty-four days when the consultant conducted a complex process of prognosis and treatment of multiple injuries and their associated problems. Slowly it became apparent to the doctors and to Stephen's wife that the treatment was both expensive and a striving officiously to keep life going at all costs. After a prolonged period of discussion and conversation it was decided to withdraw treatment and Stephen died peacefully on the fifty-fifth day in the intensive care bed.

- **A Multi-Disciplinary Team Meeting in a Cardiac Unit**

A number of doctors, nurses and others are gathered to discuss the present situation with regard to the waiting list of patients for a heart transplant. All the patients on this list are critically ill and the combination of circumstances (available organs) and finance means that not all patients will be able to have the life-saving operation. The Team, therefore, have to make a number of judgments about priorities based on the following criteria: likely outcome; the present critical health of the patient and the effects of waiting upon their condition; the matching of organs with recipients.

★

Ethics has been described as the categorizing of particular emphases, values and concerns; a framework within which a world view and vision of time enable the individual and group to understand intents and purposes, and thereby estimate the consequences of actions. Within this framework, individual and corporate needs are articulated so that in the process of rationalization we can choose between right and wrong. One view of ethics develops an appreciation and understanding of community as a place that is guided by institutions, both professional and social, whose function is to establish conventions that embody expectations, impose limitations and, ultimately, liberate. These ideals need to be worked out in the everyday business of deciding and making choices.

In relation to Sarah and Matthew the issue is that of the right to die, which has gained a considerable amount of attention in relation to attitudes to suicide, euthanasia and hunger strikes. Whose rights ought to be safeguarded and how far are individuals' sense of their rights to be influenced by others? Related to this is the issue of how far autonomy can be the determining factor in making ethical choices. In other words, how does responsibility relate to rights in relation to Sarah's child or Matthew? If there is a decision to withdraw treatment from Matthew or discontinue any treatment for Sarah's child, what is the basis on which that decision is made? We all die, so the real issue is one of control; that is, when, if and how one dies and who should decide. Related to this point is the wider question of who is to control modern illness and death, and how far medicine has over-stretched its prolonging of life at all costs. Could Matthew be allowed to live out his dying, or, put another way, just because his life in a particular form can be prolonged through the techniques of modern medicine, is this sufficient basis for prolonging it?

There are no easy solutions to the situation of Sarah and her child. There is conflict in that Sarah believes that her child should be allowed to die and the doctors want to take the opportunity to treat him, particularly as the 30% chance of surviving is significant. Her consultant believes that not to treat the child would in itself be an act of killing, and that the chance of success should persuade in favour of the radiotherapy. The consultant's senior registrar, however, finds it difficult to contradict his superior but really wants to talk through the issue of whether the radiotherapy sessions constitute ordinary or extraordinary treatment. With regard to the possibly painful medical intervention, he is of the opinion that it would be extraordinary treatment and feels more in sympathy with Sarah than his colleague. Here is a clear conflict of opinions: whose wishes are to be respected? Should the child be asked? Should the doctor's or the mother's choice be the deciding factor? Perhaps more significantly, what is the process by which the decision should be made and what is the relationship between the weighing up of the medical facts and issues related to the quality of life for the child and mother?

In a situation like Matthew's, many people affirm that the medical knowledge is uncertain. For example, it is unclear whether or not a person in the state called PVS can actually think. In this kind of case there is not always complete clarity about what constitutes brain death. The normal criteria are an absence of eye opening, no verbal response and a loss of brain stem reflexes. If these criteria are met then there is good evidence to suggest that there is irreversible brain damage and therefore profound dysfunction. However, if the patient's cortex is intact it is possible that they experience things around them and understand what is being said, but have lost their motor function. Nevertheless, PVS is an irreversible coma and it is impossible for the person to be kept alive without direct medical intervention. If the purpose of medical intervention and life-saving treatment is to benefit the patient or effect changes for the better, how does this relate to the prolonging of life for Matthew? Should Matthew continue to be fed or not and where should society draw the line? Would ceasing to treat Matthew be killing him or letting him go? What is life – a beating heart or a self-sufficient being?

The issue of the process by which decisions are made comes to the forefront for Doreen. There are tensions and difficulties between the nurse and the doctor as the issue of the relationship between cure and care is worked out through choices and decisions to be made in the case. The doctor is in a difficult situation in so far as it is not always easy to ascertain the truth about the prognosis of this cancer. Perhaps doctors are forced into giving a prognosis when they would rather not do it, and indeed might be criticized for hiding behind statistics which lead to an unhelpful over-optimism. Most doctors know that the process of prognosis is an uncertain kind of science. However, while the dilemma belongs to the nurse and doctor, and in this situation they seem to be in conflict, it also belongs to the patient. One wonders where Doreen is in the choice. There are important lessons to be learnt about inter-professionalism in so far as it reflects the way in which power operates as choices and decisions are made. The doctor might argue that the decision must ultimately be his for he has responsibility for the patient. The nurse may argue that her experience, expertise and knowledge should be taken into consideration and used in the interests of the patient. This is her role as patient's advocate set against the paternalism of the doctor. In this situation, one wonders what principle should operate. Perhaps there are two lessons to be learnt. The first is that an informed decision is the correct basis for a solution. The doctor and the nurse need to be informed by the patient, the patient by the doctor, and the nurse and the doctor informed by each other, so that to-gether they can find a solution. Above all, it seems that what is needed here is a fluid attitude to what is right and what is wrong. There is always room for improvement and shared understanding as together patient and professionals work out the balance between short-term harm and long-term benefits, which are never totally clear within this area.

The situation of Stephen highlights the complexity of intensive care treatment where a number of connected and overlapping issues bear upon the situation. There are questions about the adequacy of the initial care, which seems to be related to the challenge of this kind of treatment, where diagnostic accuracy determines the particular therapeutic interventions. Any uncertainty about prognosis is likely to increase costs. There is always an issue in situations like this of how far doctors are striving officiously to keep human life going and there will be questions about costs as a factor in determining the extent of therapy. In the case of Stephen the care that he has received depended upon such a variety of matters, strategies for management, particular guidelines and protocols. The whole cost of his treatment was in the region of £120,000. In such a case, who should make the decision about the prolonging of costly intervention, the consultant or the manager? The consultant is particularly sensitive to the way in which the approach to care on the Intensive Therapy Unit demonstrates the way in which the hospital values life. It is difficult, however, to draw the boundaries and decide what finite limit to the duration of care there should be if useful life is not expected. A number of factors come into play as this issue is explored in relation to particular cases; namely, biological age, the severity of injury, the diagnosis, and the past history of the patient. Where there is an acute shortage of intensive therapy beds, the ward team have to weigh their choices against the hospital or the authority or regional strategy for the management of the severely ill. There can only be a limited number of specialized beds at any one given moment. The doctor still wonders what the relationship is between facilitating death or stopping treatment; but above all, for him, the operation of power as it relates to choice making is important. He knows that ethical problems rarely have straightforward solutions and that by the very definition of dilemma it is impossible to define a course of action as either definitely right or completely wrong. Within this discourse his experience teaches him that there is a tendency either to simplify solutions or to generalize.

The situation faced by the Health Service in relation to Roger and the choices to be made by the team in the Cardiac Unit relate again to the whole question of priorities in health care rationing. Resources have always been limited within the National Health Service and therefore decisions about priorities – who should be treated and who should wait – have always been made. This is a complex area in debate and discussion about the Service. It is an issue which is political in so far as it relates to the level of funding of the Health Service. It is an issue that is public and corporate in so far as it relates to public expectation about health-care. The complexity for Health Service managers arise out of the measurement of outcomes as they relate to the decisions about making clinical priorities. For example, should there operate a system of informal age limits for renal dialysis or cardiac care? What are the implications for doctor-patient relationships if an aspect of the basis of the decision is financial? If there is significant public outrage at Roger's inability to have an intensive therapy bed within London, would they be prepared to increase public spending on the Health Service to accommodate this shift in expectation for this treatment? Which public expectations for health and care are realistic and reasonable and which are not? What seems important in both of these situations is that we should be able to understand the criteria behind such decisions and that these criteria should be applied with justice within a transparent national policy. In this important sense issues and choices about health care rationing ought to be debated in such a way that the clashes of personal and social values are made explicit and a community works together towards a framework of guiding principles. The tension is between limited resources and standards of care. Doctor Calman, the Government's Chief Medical Officer, offered his own guiding principle: 'What would I do if this were my mother wanting treatment?' While this may affirm the importance of seeing people's lives as at the heart of the decision making process, it is surely impossible to fulfil all our needs. Health Service managers have to deploy limited resources. The questions are what and who influences these decisions, and how far costs are to be the basis for choice? Further, what scope have local populations for influencing and challenging these decisions?

A number of important questions and issues emerge from the encounter with these ethical issues and questions. The first, and undergirding one, relates to the sheer diversity of perspective. Problems in ethics are not the same for everyone. For example, the assertion implicit in many of the stories, that it is of fundamental importance to maximize patient autonomy, is a good deal more difficult both in theory and practice than may appear at first sight. It is simply true that there are systematic differences in the way different disciplines approach the problem, and if patient autonomy is to be maximized this will require massive professional co-operation and a readiness not to retreat behind discipline barriers. The particular power relationship between nurse and doctor seems fundamental here. If there are systematic differences in the way that professions approach issues, it would seem mistaken to allow one discipline's understanding and perspective, usually the doctor's, to stand for everyone's. Perhaps those involved in the training of health care professionals in ethics ought to do this on a multi-disciplinary basis. There is much to be learnt as men and women operate, often, with different ethical systems. Some authors in the nursing field have distinguished nurses as having a particular ideology of caring, whereas doctors supposedly have one of curing. Might it be indicative that hospital medicine continues to be male-dominated and nursing female-dominated? Carol Gilligan writes with force in this area giving empirical evidence suggesting that boys approach ethical conflicts in terms of somewhat pat, mathematically quantifiable solutions, whereas girls are more likely to see all sides and find resolution more difficult. For example, when an 11 year-old boy was asked, 'When one's responsibility to oneself and responsibility to others is in conflict, how should one choose?', he replied with incredible brevity: 'You go about 1/4 to the others and 3/4 to yourself'. When asked the same question, a girl of the same age offered a long and detailed reply, weighing up both sides of the situation with feeling and subtlety.

The mode used here of focussing ethical conversation around real situations and stories is gaining authority within many educational institutions. There is an artificiality in dealing with or teaching ethics as a subject when it becomes separate and distinct from everyday action. For example, in Birmingham there are numerous studies of the allocation of treatment against a background of scarce medical resources, but few on the allocation of nurse time. The point here is that too often the doctor dominates the conversation and the issues become divorced from the challenges and pressures of the process of delivering care. The way nurse time is used on the ward area is of fundamental importance to the model, philosophy and approach to care. Too often the nurses' perspective is not valued or listened to, as the prevailing philosophy has been too ready to accept a medical orientation as alone carrying weight.

Another theme that emerges in our encounter is the preparedness to deal with risk and uncertainty. Doing everything right in ethical terms can, nevertheless, lead to unhappy endings. Sometimes it is not clear what the right solution or answer is, and there is a need to tolerate a diversity of approaches and uncertainty over which is the most desirable outcome. Patients often fail to understand that health care professionals are unable to provide a risk-free environment. Some risk is unavoidable whatever the option and therefore the health care institution and environment need to tolerate uncertainty and risk. This is why there needs to be some multi-disciplinary realism in the process of making decisions and choices.

Some particularly interesting questions are raised by the on-going work in relation to transplantation surgery. Here again, there are no easy answers, but attention needs to be given to what kind of questions frame our thinking and action. There are some arguments in relation to transplantation that are not raised or discussed as often as they might be. Perhaps the assumption that all organ transplantation is right needs some further challenging and discussion. This relates, in part but not wholly, to the issue of finance. Organ transplantation is expensive. Could the money be used to treat more people with a greater guarantee of success? By offering cardiac or liver transplantation are we raising expectations of prolonging life beyond what is reasonable? Should the money for these expensive operations be used to develop primary or community health care services? This is a fundamental resourcing issue that challenges the very fabric of the organization of Western health care systems, and indeed the distribution of wealth. While there is an attractiveness about the short-term radical redistribution solutions, and while the new procedures may be initially expensive, this may be a necessary part of the price paid for progress. It is often interesting to listen to health care professionals involved in transplantation work talk about what they themselves would do if placed in that particular situation as patients. Often they give voice to the fear that they would not go through with transplantation because the trauma is too great. The quality of life during the assessment, the transplant and the post-transplant period can often be quite appalling; where people live with constant uncertainty and can die without dignity or the appropriate preparation. Professionals can see and have to cope with relationships that this situation has strained, with lost employment and other social problems. However, this needs to be balanced against the successful transplantation cases, where many families know that it is their choice whether to take the risks and they do so because their desire to live is so great. Their experience is often that they can grow closer during the time of their trauma and find new meaning and purpose through it. Their quality and quantity of life are enhanced.

Does the multi-disciplinary team meeting in the Cardiac Unit perhaps never take a step back to view what they are doing within this wider perspective? Perhaps their decision making would be enhanced by asking some fundamental questions: for example, what are the motives underlying the development of organ transplantation? What are the values underlying it; and who gains and who loses by organ transplantation? Above all, in the process of decision making, are the views on a particular subject based on reasoned and informed argument or on motive response? While the desire to save life and increase knowledge in the search for the prevention and cure of disease gives the staff involved enormous personal and professional fulfilment, there are important questions to ask about the value of life. Should life be prolonged at all costs, and is the refusal to accept suffering, death and dying as part of life acceptable or reasonable? It is often impossible to measure the quality of life of supposed 'successes'; and it is important to question the priority of crisis and interventionist medicine over community or preventative health provision.

Another theme undergirding this discussion concerns the relationship between cost consciousness and care within the Health Service. Can all of our expectations around health be necessarily fulfilled? People often despair of the increased attention given, as a result of the government reforms in health care during the 1990s, to finance efficiency and effectiveness. All those involved in health care are faced with particular dilemmas about using money to the greatest advantage. It is important to have a costing system whereby those who have to choose know the relative cost of a particular treatment and its possible outcomes. Government reforms in this respect have been ethically innovative in separating the commissioning or purchasing of health care from its provision. This has been ethically innovative in that it has sought to transfer power away from those with vested interests in the maintenance of clinically interesting domains (that is powerful doctors) toward those with a more global outlook. It is now less easy, if not impossible, for clinicians to appropriate resources, and it is more possible for managers and health purchasers to enable resources to be directed to those in need. The main ethical difficulty here, however, is that we shall continue to face the necessity of rationing services and care, because the National Health Service will remain a service in which a limited volume of resources has to be allocated among a plethora of competing needs – not all of which can be met. One of the exciting things about the reforms is that the stages of the rationing process (which has always happened) may become more visible and therefore more open to contestation. As the public is allowed access to the contracts between purchasers and providers they can see how purchasers decide on their priorities. These ethical choices can be debated, discussed, shared and understood. It may be possible for a given community to say to their purchasing authority how they wish money to be spent. Pressure groups can influence the direction of resources according to their understanding of needs.

However, the government reforms avoided the range of difficult issues relating to rationing by perpetuating the myth that the National Health Service proceeds on the basis of planning for need. As health care has developed, the service in fact forwent the luxury of believing that it was planning for need over twenty years ago, when the realization could no longer be avoided that it was impossible to satisfy everybody's needs for health care. The real issue became (and still is) how to spread fixed and finite resources: put another way, the meeting of needs has given way to the rationing of resources. So the pretence that a tax-funded health care service can and should provide everything from cosmetic surgery to life-extending treatments must sooner or later be looked in the face. Our National Health Service, funded as it is, cannot deliver all forms of health care at an acceptable standard. Choices are inescapable, about what is to be provided, to whom and by what standard. At present such choices are exercised largely behind the veil of clinical autonomy and sooner or later we must face the exciting time when explicit distinctions are made between core services and secondary services. If so, a public stage must be prepared upon which the ethical arguments can be rehearsed.

It is not easy to see a way through this territory towards a likely consensus. Perhaps theology has a part to play in the formation of a mindset of socially radical communities that can challenge the contentions and values of the prevailing culture. Perhaps the church might recover its subversive role to influence politics and values in the process of conversation and discussion or at least keep issues of value on the agenda. What is needed above all is continued work at exploring the values that undergird these choices, and at determining what kind of morality can change our world for the better. In this sense ethics and spirituality belong together as they shape the context of our understanding of freedom and truth. This conversation is in essence theological, as Christians have long experience of the relevant questions and an underlying appreciation of life in the light of a particular view of the world and understanding of the purpose of human existence. Detailed Christian ethics rooted in the command to love, is mediated through the emotional and the dynamic rather than the purely rational as it works towards decisions or counsel. Ethics therefore becomes a way of responding to human encounters, not simply a set of dilemmas to be resolved at a rational distance. Ethical discussion is about discovery and helping people to make their own enquiry and judgments. What undergirds it is an appeal to what is best in all of us, and a vision that can inspire love and move toward the realizing of human potential.

7

Caring, Curing and Learning:

Exploring the agencies and institutions of health care

- **Anne**

I am a business manager for cardiac services in a large Acute Unit in the East Midlands. I manage a budget of £22 million pounds with my clinical colleague, a senior cardiac surgeon with a national reputation for transplant surgery. My job is clear: to manage cardiac services to the highest possible standard within the available resources. It is a competitive environment so I have to ensure that waiting lists are kept down to comply with national targets set by the Department of Health and that we have the staffing level to allow the beds to be open for a steady through-put of patients. This meets the requirements of the contracts that are placed with us by a number of purchasing organizations. I appreciate that beyond my concern for bed numbers, completed consultant episodes and finance there are other concerns relating to both staff and patients, but my primary responsibility is the effective use of resources, in promoting our unit as an attractive and cost-efficient place for cardiac medicine and surgery.

- **James**

I am a practice development nurse working with nurses in a teaching hospital to improve and develop nursing care. I provide short courses so that nurses can come together to reflect on their experience and have their knowledge base updated to improve their nursing practice. I work particularly with nursing auxiliaries, many of whom have come into nursing in their middle years with very valuable life experience. This experience is a marvellous resource for learning and makes possible a sensitive nursing response to the care of people in our ward areas.

• Helen

I am a 44 year-old woman with a husband who works away from home and two lovely children aged 14 and 10. Two weeks ago I discovered a small lump in my breast and I went to my GP who referred me to the local hospital. I went on my own to the consultation and I can't begin to describe my feelings of terror and anxiety. The consultant examined me and said that he wanted to draw some fluid off. He told me what the test was for and where they would put the needle. If I'd known what I was going to have to go through, I would have brought someone with me. I didn't know what was going to happen. I didn't know it was going to be a general anaesthetic. The consultant made it seem so minor. I hadn't even made the arrangements to be off work the next day.

I waited ten days for the results, which I thought was too long. I assumed because it was so long that it wasn't cancer. I got a telephone call from the hospital and went into the Out Patients Department. The nurse asked me to take off my clothes. I was there stripped off: I had my top off for twenty minutes. I sat shivering, thinking 'Have I got it or not?'

The surgeon who spoke to me was obviously a very clever man but he couldn't really talk to me. He told me I had breast cancer and did not say much else. I was so shocked, I didn't ask him any questions. He told me I was going to have a mastectomy. No choice, no explanation. They give the impression they're experts and know what they are doing.

I left shocked and wandered around town in a daze. I'll never forget that day and those feelings.

• Martin

I am a senior lecturer in surgery in a University Department of Surgery based in a large Acute Teaching Hospital. I specialize in surgery of the stomach and colon. I have a dual responsibility for working with both patients and students. I expend a great deal of effort and care in developing my skill and understanding as a surgeon and delight in the opportunity to teach. My ambition is to become Professor of Surgery, either in this country or in America. My first book is due to be published this year and I am working on my thesis, which I hope will make a very significant contribution to knowledge in my field.

- **Marion**

I am approaching retirement, having worked as a nurse for the past thirty-five years. I worked as a ward sister in my local hospital before I took some time off to raise my family. When the time came for me to return to nursing I did some further training and became a district nurse. I work around the Kidderminster and Stourbridge area in the town and the country. My job is more than work to me; it's a real part of my life. I love the privilege of being able to care for my patients who are part of my extended family. It's a varied and challenging life and I especially pride myself on working with my GPs to ensure that people are treated as individuals and are kept in their home environment wherever possible. I feel this is especially important for older people. I am not going to find it easy to retire and regret some of the changes in the Health Service. I'm especially sorry that so many nurses seem to feel that their work is a job and not a vocation.

- **Roger**

I am a doctor working in a hospice with people living with terminal disease. I have never felt so fulfilled as a doctor. The team here work together to care for the person, their families and the range of physical and non-physical challenges that terminal illness presents. I am learning so much about the meaning of pain and how to treat it; knowing when to withdraw and allow others in and, particularly, to appreciate the limitations of medication and medical science.

- **Celia**

  I am a social worker in a hospital working with a team to ensure that care packages are delivered to patients so their social needs for care are met. This may mean sorting out benefits, but, particularly, organizing, with other members of the care-team, the physical resources needed for discharge from hospital to home. The more experience I have in this setting the more I realize how varied and complex people's needs are, but especially, how interrelated and connected a person's social, emotional and physical needs can be. We sometimes fail to see the individual in context and to understand them beyond their immediate illness.

- **Kay**

  I am a newly qualified nurse on a busy surgical ward in a general hospital. I find it hard to describe the reasons why I went into nursing; it was a kind of intuition, a strong intuition that this kind of work would give me fulfilment and satisfaction. I enjoyed my training and particularly the way in which we had such a variety of experiences of different kinds of health care. I particularly enjoyed my placement on a surgical ward and decided to apply for my present post in the light of this. I got on well with the ward sister and some of the others in the team and I am very stimulated by the activity and busyness of the ward. In this kind of work you see the results very quickly. Patients go for their operation and one is part of the process of healing as the wounds are dealt with and a patient is slowly encouraged to walk and recover. I can't imagine another job where I'd have so much contact with a wide variety of people. The amazing thing is that these people share so much of their thoughts and their lives with me and I enjoy listening to them. We have had a few deaths on the ward and a couple of the older nurses feel that I need to be careful not to get over-involved with the patients. The doctors vary a lot – at the moment I get on really well with the two house officers. The consultants pop in and out of the ward and it feels to me that they are very much in charge of what happens.

• Michael

I am a member of a very active evangelical church which brought me to faith and continues to keep my discipleship nurtured and challenged. I belong to a local prayer group which meets every month to pray for the sick and to plan our quarterly healing service. During this service, along with the other ministers, I partake in the 'laying on of hands' and I feel part of the church's commitment to health and healing. I try as far as I am able to support the doctors and nurses that belong to my local congregation.

I had cause to visit my local GP recently with a persistent trouble with some stomach pains. I remember the visit was surrounded with a great deal of anxiety but once I was in the consulting room I felt reassured by my doctor's expertise. I was confident that he knew how to diagnose my problem and treat it as quickly and efficiently as possible.

*

Anne raises a number of interesting questions and dilemmas. One wonders, with her, about the nature of control within the financing of health care. How does she maintain integrity between the task of balancing her financial resources and the reality that the activity focusses on human beings, often at their most vulnerable and in acute need? Perhaps few patients understand the real constraints that managers have to operate under. There seems to be a clear need for information about the basis on which decisions are made. For James the experiential learning becomes an exciting opportunity to improve and develop models of health care. He hopes that through his work many of the life experiences of older nurses might be used to improve the way in which the nursing team plans for care. He believes that the reforms have provided the institution of the hospital with unique opportunities to rethink patterns of care. The necessary challenging and the asking of questions as a culture changes is, for James, a positive element of development.

While much work has been done to improve the way in which information is shared, and Helen may represent only a small minority of people, she does give voice to an important experience of the patient within an institution of health care. It would be impossible to alleviate all anxiety; but the surgeon needs to re-evaluate radically how he shares information with his patients. As one reflects on Helen's situation alongside an appreciation of the energy and skill of Martin, it seems sensible not to expect too much from doctors. How far can the surgeon both be an expert with the knife and sensitively attune himself to some of the human elements of care and relationship?

Marion and Roger give voice to two varied reflections of alienation and discontentment with the present culture of the Health Service. Marion regrets a golden past when nurses often viewed their work more as a vocation than a job. It would be interesting to ask both Marion and Roger how they view the nature of professionalism, and how far the professional boundaries set up as medicine and nursing have developed, empower sensitive, engaged care. Roger especially represents many doctors who feel that the culture of institutional medicine does not provide the conditions in which they can work creatively for the patient.

Despite the considerable development of hospice care and critiques of medicine within this country and abroad, few of these insights seem to have been integrated into developing new models of care in hospital.

Celia's role in a hospital is very significant as she can be the key person to facilitate an effective discharge. She has an appreciation of the complex nature of people's needs and how they are interrelated, though she feels that the medical model of disease does not help to provide a structure around which an approach to whole person care might be made possible. For Kay it is the task orientated nature of surgical nursing that gives her a sense of satisfaction. Her strength is to be able to perform a multiplicity of physical tasks for the patient with speed and skill. She, like Martin, may find herself at a loss to spend more time at the bed-side listening and supporting.

Michael gives voice to faith both in his church and in Christian discipleship but also in his GP. One wonders how these two relate and where and who is the agent of health and healing for Michael in his exploration of his stomach pains.

The concepts of cure, care and teaching lie at the heart of a large city teaching hospital. As an institution it has a culture that undergirds its work and influences the experience of health care. As it is a teaching hospital, the connections between caring, curing and learning are obvious for nurses, medical students, physiotherapists, occupational therapists, speech therapists and other health care professionals. Within this culture there are a number of models and concepts of health that are reflected in the individuals and professions described above. This chapter will attempt to explore the agencies and institutions of health care as they are reflected in the people heard above who approach health from such different perspectives and places.

The clearest influence on the understanding of professional training for healthcare is the notion of health as 'an absence of disease'. This notion is often taken for granted in official medical publications and has dominated Western thinking about health during the past two centuries. This is often termed the *medical model* and is linked to the rise during the last century of the scientific investigation of disease by a growing body of specialist doctors and researchers, and to the emergence of health work as a formal professionalized area of expertise. Within this view, health is viewed as both the absence of disease and as functional fitness. Health Services are geared mainly towards treating sick and disabled people and a high value is put on the provision of specialist medical services, in mainly institutional settings. Within the *medical model* doctors and other qualified experts diagnose disease and sanction and supervise the withdrawal of patients from productive labour. The function of the Health Service as an institution and agency is remedial and curative. Disease and sickness are explained within a biological framework that emphasizes the physical nature of disease. In the treatment of illness it takes a biologically reductionist view of the person. A high value is put on using scientific methods of research and on scientific knowledge. This is the model of health within which Martin the lecturer in surgery works and, interestingly, the model that Michael, despite his beliefs, assents to in his reflection about his expectations of his doctor. Kay, the nurse, finds herself often disempowered by working within this framework as she puts into practice the wishes of the doctor and consultant.

In 1974 the World Health Organization defined health in the following way:

Health is not merely the absence of disease, but a state of complete physical, mental, spiritual and social wellbeing.

This definition builds a positive vision of health as comprehensive wellbeing, in which preoccupation with disease is replaced by a recognition of the framework of individual health. It reflects a critical evaluation of the *medical model* by researchers inside and outside medicine, and questions how far diseases can be objective categories and measurable entities rather than reflecting mental and social categorizations, a wide range of factors.

A definitive or even indicative account of the factors that have shaped medicine in the United Kingdom has yet to be written, but it may be worthwhile within this discussion to reflect upon some of the influences that have shaped modern medicine. There appears to be some considerable sense of crisis in medicine today as it continues to attract suspicion and criticism. This crisis needs to be set against the innovative and life-changing effects that medicine has had over the last fifty years. Amongst these innovations include the discovery and development of penicillin, antibiotics, steroids, transplants and other surgery. Medical science and research have transformed our understanding of the human body and consequently our ability to conquer disease. Medicine, therefore, has grown in significance and power over this period as it has transformed our lives. Society, in turn, has invested an enormous amount in medicine as a social utility and good.

Despite this, however, medicine continues to be fundamentally challenged by a number of groups and individuals. These challenges include the evidence adduced by critics like McKeown who have shown that medicine is not all that effective compared to other agencies and can sometimes do positive harm. Thus life expectancy has increased this century because of improved living standards and not the development of medical expertise. This point is made by P. D. James in her novel *The Children of Men*:

> Western science has been our god. In the variety of its power it has preserved, comforted, healed, warmed, fed and entertained us and we have felt free to criticize and occasionally reject it as men have always rejected their gods, but in the knowledge that despite our apostasy, this deity, our creature and our slave, would still provide for us; the anaesthetic for the pain, the spare heart, the new lung, the antibiotic, the moving wheels and the moving pictures. The light will always come on when we press the switch and if it doesn't we can find out why . . . for all our knowledge, our intelligence, our power, we can no longer do what the animals do without thought. No wonder we both worship and resent them (pp. 5–6).

There has been a cultural challenge by many individual lay people and pressure groups in our pluralistic culture who have come to think that there is a wider and more valued health care market than has been supposed, and even much conventional medicine might fail to promote health. This will be explored later. There have been professional challenges by other groups such as nurses who argue that they can do things that make for health better than doctors and for less money. This point was made in a discussion between a group of nurses and doctors in a teaching hospital. When asked what they would most like to change about doctors, nurses replied, 'their power, they are too powerful'. To this challenge the doctors' response was 'we are powerful because we have the ultimate responsibility'. There has also been an organizational challenge by government which is tempted to tame medical power and to ensure the effective use of money and resources in an organizational shift of power from the doctor to the general manager.

The World Health Organization has had a very important influence as it has been able to build up a wider picture of medicine's recent history and what problems and difficulties face it in the next millennium. Statistics show a dual (and paradoxical) challenge to human society that has given increased significance to medicine. The world's population has doubled because of medicine's interventions and preventions, while at the same time medicine has acquired the ability to prevent a population explosion through the introduction of the contraceptive pill. There has been a therapeutic revolution which, however, coincides with the reality that medicine has been more open to criticism and also has had to deal with setbacks and failures. Research, for example, on cancer or Alzheimer's disease, creeps along very slowly and HIV disease has posed considerable challenges to the ability of medicine to deal with disease. Culturally society seems divided between affirming medicine as a profession with prestige and power, and questioning whether medicine is in fact able to be all-conquering and in command of disease.

The development of medical sociology in the 1950s has challenged the professional dominance of medicine for the way that it has defined notions of health and sickness within particular modes of social control and the reproduction of social norms (see chapter 4). Sociologists like Roy Porter have questioned the power-base of the profession and argued that medicine has become a prisoner of its own success. This surely compels medicine to rethink what its aims and objectives are.

It is interesting also to note the politicization of medicine. The British health care system has been moulded by the values, cultural norms and institutions prevailing in the modern nation state. The creation of the health care system in 1948 was, perhaps in part, a design to complement Britain's big-power status and a part of the British empirical and utilitarian tradition. The nineteenth-century industrial and urban legacy and two world wars left Britain with the determination to expand education and to improve health, as essential parts of an improved quality of life. The health and welfare services offered opportunities for a redistribution of wealth and a reduction of inequality. Still today we struggle with this challenge. Although the National Health Service absorbs so much state funding, the proportion of the national expenditure has always been low. Perhaps, therefore, from the very establishment of the Health Service, medicine was never allowed to succeed in meeting the expectations directed towards it.

Set against this background it is difficult not to have sympathy with the agenda of the Thatcherite determination to use resources more effectively and efficiently and to decrease state intervention as a market-place approach was offered to the public as the consumer of these goods. While there was considerable opposition to the reforms from the medical profession, it has since 1990 implemented the changes with considerable vigour and energy combined with a lack of critical reflectiveness about some of the fundamental questions about medicine that have been outlined. It remains to be seen whether the government will allow the market in health care to run and operate freely and indeed, if they do, whether GPs or hospitals will be the monopoly supplier of the commodity of health. Further, if the citizen is the consumer of health it remains to be seen whether or not many will continue to work for a style of medicine that treats them more humanely and holistically. Women have been particularly successful in challenging the approach and organization of children's and maternity services, as it has been argued that it is wrong to medicalize normal life events. There is a more vocal assertion of the claim that patient autonomy ought to be cherished and safeguarded wherever possible.

The critique of the *medical model* of health continues apace. However, both politics and medicine have failed to address the paradox that an increased health status in the population has led to an increased craving for medicine. Does medicine collude with the general public's expectation that all can be cured, in a 'can do must do' medical approach to issues? Can medicine fulfil the increased demand of medical consumerism, where life is extended for the sake of it and expectations are advanced to a point where they are unrealizable? The present approach makes a cash limit on health resources and this will continue to force medicine to redefine what its limits are. In this process of redefinition, medicine will have to explore the interrelationship between money, power, knowledge and practice if it is to retain its influence.

Over the past twenty years this critique of the *medical model* of health has gradually moved opinion towards what has been defined as a *social model* of health. This emphasizes the environmental causes of health and disease, and in particular makes the connection between individuals and their environment as a dynamic interaction. Many health researchers have argued that the business of improving health needs to address all these four fields: human biology, life-style, environment and health care organization. This emphasizes the wider natural, social, economic and political setting within which health or disease is experienced. It is the model of health familiar to Cecilia, the social worker who knows from her own personal and professional experience that the factors affecting a person's health are many and varied and that therefore the restoration to health must address these wider social factors. Marion, the district nurse, also knows from her personal experience how far life-style and environment impinge upon a person's experience of health. Unlike Kay, the hospital nurse, she sees people in their normal contexts and understands some of the wider dimensions of their living. James is part of the considerable developments that have been taking place in nursing over the past three decades as nurses begin to take a greater place in the organization and delivery of health care. The nursing profession has consolidated and developed its expertise and the indications are that its members will continue to want to exercise more power in the organization and delivery of health care at a number of levels, both within hospitals and in the community.

A person's own beliefs about health and illness are connected to wider social, cultural and material factors. The views that we collect will be influenced to varying degrees by age, sex, occupation and so on. Social background and material circumstances, education and cultural affiliations may be important too. It is clear therefore that if a person's health chances are dependent upon a wide variety of factors, then promotion of health means addressing significant inequalities, both within society and in the agencies and institutions of health care. For example, the DHSS Report on *Inequalities in Health*, the work of a committee chaired by Sir Douglas Black in 1980, disclosed, amongst other things, that there were marked differences in mortality rates between occupational groups. It showed that long-standing illness is twice as common in lower social groups than in professional groups. It argued that there were inequalities in the utilization of medical services, especially of the preventative services, with severe under-utilization by the working classes, and that differences in material living conditions are the most significant factor that gives rise to differences in physical and mental health. These challenges to the conventional view of promotion of health have resulted in some radical changes in perspective about what agencies and institutions make for health care, and now a full range of forces can be brought to bear.

This admission of the diverse and complex nature of 'health chances' is bound up with an understanding of the nature of what has been termed *quality of life*. Both Marion and Celia know that an individual's quality of life is dependent upon a wide range of factors, some of which we have no power to change. Life is shaped both by our physical and mental wellbeing, and by our socio-economic status and the quality of the environment. Our personal space, income, standard of living, occupation and warmth have the power to determine the quality of our lives. Cultural factors such as age, gender, class, race and religion are also important influences that shape our health. More intangible factors, such as social integration (social and family factors, social roles), purposeful activity (recreation, work, other interests) and expressed satisfaction (self-image and sense of fulfilment) also play their part in the overall picture. These developments in the understanding of health needs have formed the modern understanding of how we should organize and deliver health care in a variety of settings. They have also shaped professional training.

Not surprisingly, until recently not only practice but also much of nurse training and education reflected the *medical model* of health. This structured health professionals' thinking about practice – about their patients and about health services – and marginalized other approaches. Now, many hospital and community nurses have been seeking to distance themselves from medical control and identify the particular skills, knowledge and under-pinning philosophy of nursing. One of the main forces impelling Project 2000 and numerous diploma and degree programmes has been the growing realization that as long as nurses were trained to work within the *medical model*, the skills required within contemporary nursing practice (for example, to work in teams and to control sophisticated technology) would not receive much public recognition or occupational reward. From this angle too the *social model* of health has come to prominence.

While this model has shaped nurse training, there continue to be some significant problems with the culture of medicine and areas where the more comprehensive model has made scarcely any headway. In her experiences Helen feels the effects of a medical culture which is insensitive to her wider emotional and spiritual needs. Roger, as a hospice doctor, finds a culture where a group of health care professionals can work together for the patient and which stands in sharp contrast to his hospital experience. The social model of health, therefore, challenges much of the contemporary culture of the hospital in its thinking and practice and communal being.

It is important, however, to appreciate the fundamental changes that have taken place within the organization and provision of health care in Britain. Some of these changes have been driven by the necessity to look carefully at the ways in which money is spent on health, but it has also been influenced by developments in clinical practice, shorter lengths of stay in hospital, the provision of more care and treatment in the community and people's developing interest in their own health needs. For many years the focus of health care as an agency and institution has been on hospitals, with the agencies of primary care in the community regarded as satellites of these powerful institutions. What is significant today is that primary health care in the community is increasingly becoming the focus for improving health as the *social model* of health begins to affect the culture, agency and institutions of health care. It is against this background of improving and developing primary care that the churches need to explore the appropriate models of health care work, moving away from the traditional emphasis on hospitals as the primary location.

To summarize therefore: there has been a growth in the recognition of the contribution of different skills to the common task of providing health care. However, there continue to be considerable difficulties in the implementation of this *social model* of health. Part of the problem lies with the fact that many senior doctors have not fully absorbed the new model. Martin's skills work within a very particular area of medicine: what and how would his understanding of a wider *social model* of health contribute to his work as a surgeon? Perhaps it might affect the way Helen was treated, or affirm the social worker's place in an interdisciplinary approach to health-care. Kay, the nurse, may appreciate the *social model* of health but the great (*too* great for many?) demands, humanly and psychologically, of this model limit her work and her role. Perhaps there are problems of over-involvement with people's whole 'worlds'. Can one expect busy doctors to be suitably competent to meet such demands? In other words there are real problems and difficulties in the movement away from the *medical model* towards the *social model* of health. These difficulties lie, not least, with the expectations of patients like Michael, who have very particular hopes from their doctor. Perhaps all that can be hoped is continued articulation of the dilemmas and issues of working within particular cultures of health care for both patient and professional.

What are the theological principles involved in developing new agencies and institutions of health care? What dimensions of thinking might Michael's church reflect upon as they look at health and healing at the local church? The theological principles follow and undergird thinking about the *social model* of health. This insists on the interconnectedness between the various aspects of the person and between human beings and their environment. It follows, therefore, that where the *medical model* of health predominates, hospital institutions especially are likely to employ a narrow concept of health and disease that can often fail to explore and respond to the reality of these interconnections. Concern for health is contained within the affirmation of faith in the goodness of God upon which we all depend, and in his beneficent purpose of human fulfilment, expressed traditionally in the idea of the creation of the human race in the divine image. It is manifested in his grace in the gifts and abilities he has given to people to enable ill health to be prevented and the sick to be restored. Within this context the concern for health involves tolerating uncertainty, taking risks and making mistakes which are to be regarded as stepping stones in our shared search for wholeness. The church has a particular perspective on this search, involving a readiness to work with concepts such as sin and salvation, despair and hope; to take seriously both malevolence and benevolence, doom and rescue; and to know the difference between human arrogance and creatureliness. The Christian's incarnational faith creates a constant bias towards seeing persons as wholes, rather than as, for example, purely physical organisms.

We have noted that health and disease are parts of a social process with moral, ethical and financial aspects. If society is to pay due attention to this process and these dimensions in considering how best to promote wellbeing in the community, there is room for the church to play its part, not least in exploring what it means to be human and to have health in and through community. Perhaps above all it can contribute by holding steady this width of considerations in the face of persistent tendencies to narrow the range of factors that are allowed to play their part. In the social organization of health problems, doctors in particular need to address the challenges posed by health and disease by sharing power, both with their colleagues and with their patients. The users of health care services need to be offered knowledge, skills and support to enable them to take an active interest in their own health and wellbeing.

The place of Christians in this debate and dialogue poses some interesting challenges and demands caution. There needs to be an admission that not all styles of Christian conviction and religious life are conducive to what is explored and encountered above. Indeed some Christian approaches may be positively harmful! For example, where there is an emphasis on Christian separateness from society in a shut-off 'religious' sphere, or on human sinfulness, or on narrow, at-all-costs evangelism. None of these approaches would affirm a style of Christian pastoral care that cares both for the person and for their world in health care.

In this important sense all churches have it in them to be a resource for health and healing. There are important historical and contemporary connections to be made between religion and medicine in both primary and secondary care. Churches should explore developing close working relationships with the local primary health care centres, health promotion units and possibly GP practices. The church can make a contribution to providing other services to aid the health community, such as befrienders, skilled listeners, baby sitters, help with transportation and legal work. Such integration affirms the importance of convictions about our deepest needs where health care is concerned. It acknowledges that the search for wholeness requires a wider model than that provided conventionally by the Health Services alone, one that involves an inner journey as well as the use of the techniques of medicine. This work, therefore, is about building healthy alliances to encourage people, both individuals and groups, to have an informed voice and reflective wisdom about their care.

8

Divine Action, Prayer and Belief:
Exploring the hope and possibility of healing

Perspectives

- It is ten o'clock in the morning and I am at work at my desk in Diocesan Church House. The telephone rings and to my surprise it is my father in extreme distress. He is ringing from the local general hospital in Durham with the news that my mother has had a heart attack and is in a serious condition in the Coronary Care Unit. My heart races and I panic – will she live? What should I do? I sort out the office, rush home and then drive north. My hope and prayer is simple: 'Please God let her live, protect and make her better.' I make my demands aloud and hope amidst my shock and tears that God will come and help. In my head I know that this desire is full of theological problems and questions but my heart wants life for my mother. In the healing debate, how does the head relate to the heart? There are two voices: one asks about the rationality of wanting God's intervention for my mother, the other is plain and insistent.

- I am called into the Intensive Care Unit at the request of a young woman's mother. The young woman is dying and the consultant has told her parents that there is nothing more they can do for her. I sit in the visitors' room and make some tea for the distressed couple. The man tells his wife, 'We have got to accept it – she has gone and we can't have her back.' 'No' comes the reply from his wife, 'I wanted the chaplain to ask the Lord to deliver my daughter from death.' For what, then, do I pray? What difference will our prayers make? How will we know they won't?

- I bump into a consultant on an oncology ward who is examining some X-rays of his patient with a group of medical students.
  He invites me to examine them. The photographs are of a man's
  lung taken a day apart. The first one shows two dark patches
  about the size of a large fist which are threatening cancer
  tumours. On the second the tumours have completely gone.
  There is no medical explanation at all. The patient had no
  treatment. The consultant joked with me, 'Have you been at
  him with prayer?!' Unfortunately I could make no claims to the
  power of my prayers and the case remains a mystery. In the
  words of the consultant, 'That has occurred in similar situations
  about four or five times in my twenty-seven years as a doctor.' Is
  it possible to explain the disappearance of the cancer? What
  kind of explanation are we to look for?

- I am present at a debate between Christians of very different
  perspectives on 'Christian Healing'. The message that challenges me is this: God heals and healing activities are in many parts
  of the churches a key element in the renewal of parish life and
  spiritual activity. Lives are changed and healed and communities are transformed through the power of prayer and this
  should be part of hospital ministry. The tradition seems clear
  but in a post-modern world how far will our Christian past take
  us? Can there be other distinctive Christian traditions about
  healing? Healing, viewed from the common perspective, is
  after all largely a modern venture. All these ancient traditions
  are perhaps obsolete from our perspective, because they
  predate modern medicine. The health care chaplain needs to
  discover what needs to be done now in the hospital and its tasks.

- I am sitting at the bedside of a patient when the consultant
  with two junior doctors visit the next bed. They are a formidable
  trio, young, male, self-assured and committed. I overhear (as
  do others within the four-bedded unit) the consultant explain
  the need for a bone marrow transplant. The disease is explained
  simply and objectively as something to be scientifically examined, treated and overcome. There appears to be no room for
  doubt or uncertainty – medicine will deal with this disease and

restore life. Can the doctor heal? Has medicine replaced theology as the science of healing? Theology was never the science of healing and doctors can be ruled by death and not by life.

★

This chapter will attempt to do two things. First, it will attempt a dialogue between the traditions and frameworks that shape our theories about health, disease and healing and some of the human experiences that refract a number of expectations, hopes, fears and realities around healing. Secondly, it will argue that those involved in health and healing need to look at more than the malfunctioning part of any person but instead need to view it from the outset as part of a person in the fullest sense, and that person as part of a community and environment. The person is to be viewed in an eschatological sense in that the reality of death and 'the end' is affirmed. Within this dialogue I am especially concerned to encourage interconnections and to uncover, where they exist, sources of integration and the areas where interpretation and connection seem impossible.

If I feel acute physical pain then it is more likely that I shall ring 999 and call for medical assistance rather than ask my parish priest for prayer and anointing. There is, of course, a long history of the priest's involvement in dying and death. From the fifth century until relatively recently, most Europeans called the priest if they thought they were dying; no doubt the agenda was the desire for a good and holy death and perhaps the fear of damnation rather than any hope of healing. The modern person experiences illness as a threat to their health and full life which can be dealt with wholly or partially by medicine administered by a scientifically trained medical profession. We value life and want to preserve it against the threat of disease. Modern medicine has distanced us and preserved us from a good deal of pain and early or 'predictable' death. We take much of it for granted as our expectations have been raised over the past two generations. My grandmother's experience of health was very different from mine today. The patient having the bone marrow transplant explained by her consultant wants medicine to preserve her life at any cost. At 38 with three young children she has much to live for.

However, when we read about illness in New Testament times and in particular traditions of the churches, as expressed in my own prayers for my mother and by the mother of the young woman dying on the Intensive Care Unit, I am reminded by fellow Christians that illness can be and is still dealt with by charismatics speaking words of power. Further, these acts of healing are sometimes effective without drugs and operation. Sometimes (though not always) faith is said to be essential. On the whole, most Christians put their trust in science and think that the New Testament stories are suspect or irrelevant. Other Christians put their trust in both; they pray with confidence for healing and blame failure on faithlessness. In the particular case, upon what does healing depend? If I pray with the parents on the Intensive Care Unit, 'Father, deliver this person from death if it is your will' and the person dies, why is our prayer ineffective? Is it? Was it God's will . . .?

Some New Testament scholars interpret the Gospel stories as pointing, even for their writers and first hearers, to *inner* attitudes, for example, not being anxious, or accepting ultimate dependence on God; or else as allegories for accepting the call to faith (the blind receive sight). In doing this they bypass the stories as history and as expressing a non-scientific mythological (and obsolete?) world view. These approaches are useful in so far as they affirm both medicine and faith as valued responses to illness. But they seem feeble or evasive alongside the evident convictions in the Gospels and those of modern believers who share them.

There are choices to be made in the way we construct our shared framework of meaning and values in relation to healing, and in our ways of acting from within it in order to promote it. Specifically, what models of God and of pastoral care undergird the practice of Christian healing?

In the scriptures there is no notion of natural law that claims to understand and determine how the universe operates necessarily along uniform lines. A miracle is described and understood as an event in which God acts in a special way in order to disclose or accomplish his purposes; and the idea of such interventions is ready to hand where scientific knowledge is so meagre. While the consultant and his junior doctors assent to a scientific framework that understands how the body functions, the doctor examining the X-rays appreciates (rather wryly) that there are events and occurrences that are beyond human understanding or explanation. Can or should the surprising disappearance of the cancer (or indeed other healings in the narrow physical sense) be understood as a violation of the laws of nature? There seems to be a limit, itself the result of a kind of pragmatism, to the lengths both doctors will go to explain what they have experienced.

It might be argued that, until the Enlightenment, most people lived in a potentially miraculous world under God's guiding and intervening hand. Since the Enlightenment the universe has come to be seen as a closed system governed by observed regularities of cause and effect. The growth and development of modern medicine is part of this world view. Yet the doctor viewing the X-rays is content to be just baffled by the spontaneous cure: for him medical knowledge is a curious mixture of knowledge and ignorance. Mystery has not been banished from our world, even though it is more marginal than it was for our ancestors.

Yet our perspectives on those Gospel healings should not be governed only by issues of historicity, that is, what actually happened. We ought also to have the creative space to explore the inner meanings of the stories, as has already been hinted. Put another way, our concern should be 'what is written *about*' rather than just 'what is written'. Take the text of the New Testament: what perspectives on healing does it give for us today? The healing events in the New Testament are set out as proof of Jesus' role in the purpose of God; of which we are today a continuing part. Healing is an indication of the presence of the Kingdom of God in which wholeness and spiritual advance take place under God's rule. For Christians, we still live under that rule, living in and for that Kingdom of Love. These matters are more fundamental and comprehensive than the question of the historicity of those stories – as indeed of the character or genuineness of their modern parallels. There is, in any case, always some sort of explanation within this world, for these are physical happenings, even if that explanation eludes us. Faith in God remains broader than such questions and is essentially unaffected by our response to them.

The challenge of how we might become the agents of healing for God remains. Jesus' method in healing was to evoke latent attitudes of faith and to link these with the healing power of God. Sometimes in the stories the faith of others is invoked to heal, so faith in the sufferer is not seen as wholly essential: we may say that healing is a shared enterprise! Jesus therefore provides an opportunity for faith and divine power to coalesce in creating a new order. Healing in the New Testament is an extraordinary event performed as a sign to the community of faith concerning God's purpose for his people.

Meanwhile the doctor's explanation of the strategy for combating the patient's disease reflects the predominant theoretical picture of the world order in relation to healing. It runs as follows: nature works according to mechanical laws and everything can be explained by logic and reason. Or perhaps doctors are more pragmatic? These procedures just *work*?! This world-view sees God (if it includes him at all) as a rather remote monarch: a transcendent being who orders everything above without any direct involvement. Indeed part of the theological traditions of the churches assents to this dualistic and deterministic world view in which everything that happens is causal. This theoretical picture is, however, often combined with mixed and confused responses when we turn to people's *actual* perceptions and responses to their sufferings and sometimes the caring professions' vicarious attitudes on the patients' behalf. So, the doctor may feel that there are times when medical knowledge is a paradoxical mixture of certainty and doubt that cannot explain or understand all experience. The doctors may feel with and for a patient in their pain and fear but cannot allow themselves to act on it or show it. The *medical model* of detachment is followed for the safety of the clear boundaries and ordered control it seems to offer. Whether it comes from doctor or from patient, perhaps the plea for salvation, for life amidst the threat and certainty of death is, in small part, assent to the intuitive feeling that there is more to health than the physical and that there are other powerful forces at work in living and healing.

A dilemma for the pastor derives from the dominant medical culture that shapes our expectations and perceptions of need. If I hesitate to pray for God to intervene and heal the parents' daughter and if I believe the doctors who are confident of the efficacy of the bone marrow transplant – what picture of God do I live by? If I then make myself comfortable by redefining some key terms which may not really engage with the raw human need as felt and expressed, does God cease to be meaningful or powerful? Is God after all neither benevolent nor, more shocking, an effective agent in the concrete events of our world? Praying seems crude if seen as representing the literal truth of the situation: perhaps prayer can be better seen as an alignment with God/the Other – placing one's situation in the divine context. Perhaps if we go further, we even demean God and reduce him to puppet-management. There is inscrutability and ultimate mystery behind all our understanding of God.

In this debate we pastors are caught up with an ongoing tension between the sacred and the secular. From the patient's perspective, however, these two may belong together: for many believe that there is a God at work in their lives and world. It looks probable that we shall have to live with the medical specialization of function which modern medicine has bred. There should though be some opportunity to bridge the gaps and failures that emerge when physicians fail to treat the emotions or spiritual capacities and environmental contexts of persons and when pastoral carers have little to do with the life of the body and its processes.

As a philosophical and theological issue, as this chapter has highlighted, the question of divine action is at the heart of the problem. Can we now see God as breaking into the sequence of cause and effect, of which we think we are aware and which seems to be the way things do and have to work? There are some theologians, for example John Polkinghorne, who have attempted to cast doubt on the prevailing popular scientific assumptions from the point of view of modern physics (Heisenberg and the uncertainty principle). Other theologians like Austin Farrer and Maurice Wiles seem less interested than the scientists in 'finding room for miracle' or explaining strange occurrences; rather they are seeking to see divine presence in 'what is'.

Much of the above concerns one aspect of the wider issue of changing ways of seeing Christian belief in the light of changing cultural assumptions: highlighted here in the matter of New Testament ideas of healing compared with modern medicine. Pastoral theologians have yet to face this issue straightforwardly and in the context of the issue of cultural change as a whole. It simply is the case that the current myth (way of picturing or telling the story) about disease and healing changes from one period to another; and while remnants of old myths lie around (or are revived, as by 'healers' of a religious kind), they are superseded for practical purposes by other myths. The Christian world at present is deeply torn between those who seek to grapple with modernity as itself God-given and those who hold on to versions (often modified or distorted) of old (especially supposed biblical) myth. Often the latter group do not fully pay the price, which would be alienation from the greater part of Western culture and intellectual life. Of course the second group is, world-wide, much more powerful in Christianity as a whole. But those who are of that persuasion are usually blithely unaware of the fact that their lives are totally based on a myth which in their religion they deny: for example, the use of modern technology, including medicine for the most part. Without realizing it, they really do live in a curiously schizoid state culturally. The problem could be dealt with by pitching the use made of the modern myth at a lower level. That is, you can say: I use modern technology and modern medicine simply because it *works* in this way and that; and I do not go further, that is, I don't bother myself about possible deep theoretical or total pictures (myths) which lie behind it. I just do this or that piece of surgery or car-repairing or computer-constructing and still believe fervently in angels and demons and God intervening in my child's examination chances or my disease. How do we bridge the total gulf between those who can bear to go on like that and those who think it will not do if integrity is to be preserved?

The question of prayer comes in again in this context. The tradition here is more complicated and interesting. It is true that intercessory prayer has overwhelmingly been modelled on the idea of a suppliant approaching a king or lord who has benefits to bestow or withhold. That model fitted very well through the greater part of the Christian period with the way the universe was seen to be run under God's direct governance, and, of course, connected with the way social and political life worked: lords – officially at least – had total power to dispose, and success consisted in getting their ear, while to lose their ear spelt disaster. Of course this might be modified by checks and balances (parliaments etc.) but it remained the underlying assumption about social relationships. So of course prayer to God followed: *and* there could be no more of a problem about failure to get answers to prayer than there could be if the lord refused to comply. You could complain, but there is no intellectual problem – it was his to give or not to give. Once divine action ceases to be seen as direct, in the old way, a problem arises; how can the thing work at all? What point can there be in asking for this and that? And if the *system* of the universe withholds goods and doles out evils, what a terrible system! So, though we go on using it in every liturgy, 'asking prayer', in this crude form and verbalized in the form of asking, is unsatisfactory. As alignment of the self with God or as placing one's affairs in the wider light of God, of 'the depth of things', prayer *in relation to* this person/situation or that makes much more sense. We may note that at the start of Christian prayer, in Matthew's version of the Lord's Prayer, asking for needs to be fulfilled is specifically ruled out as the point of it (Matthew 6.8 and 25–34). So, for Matthew, the meaning of the Lord's Prayer cannot be to seek the meeting of one's needs, but rather to desire earnestly the splendour of God's presence (kingdom). The fulfilment of God's purpose is its sole and entire content. This aspect of spirituality demands further thought and reflection for the pastoral theologian; prayer is one area where theory and practice meet.

How then should we define or understand healing? As we have seen, culture will play a significant part in shaping the ways in which we understand the process by which healing is defined.

The *Oxford English Dictionary* defines healing under four aspects:

1. To make whole or sound; to cure
2. To restore to soundness
3. To save, purify, cleanse, repair or amend
4. To become whole or sound: to recover from sickness or a wound

All four of these definitions are applicable in all cultures, so that cultural differences affect the way the processes are perceived and felt. For example, in a religious culture reconciliation to God and neighbour will be a major aspect of healing: so may the whole apparatus of 'a good death'. In a secular culture, these aspects may be subordinated or absent and the stress will be largely on physical recovery.

In the light of the above discussion I propose the following broad definition of healing: the process of being restored to wholeness, emotional well-being, mental functioning and spiritual aliveness. Healing, from the Christian viewpoint, is always linked with a spiritual advance. God is part of this process and healing or wholeness (which could be care or cure) are metaphors for religious views of salvation, which itself concerns the whole person. Therefore what healing is or means will always be an area of controversy because of the complexity of views on the nature of God and providence. In addition it will always be impossible to fully understand (as with the doctor reviewing the X-rays) the paradoxes and complexities of the human person in its totality.

So, does God act upon or against nature to heal? Perhaps there are times when God can be said to be at work in the process of making whole through a variety of agents and in ways that are both obvious and mysterious. Even if God *is not seen as acting* to heal, a religious person may still feel the God-dimension is important, even absolutely paramount: that is he or she holds to the 'ultimacy' or 'depth' in the situation and the process of healing – including its total effects for self and others.

Above all, when considering the subject of healing it will be important to understand that the theoretical 'world-fiction' of medicine is one that is held by people who are themselves, by assumption, 'healthy'. And it is far removed from the perceptions of the self as patient or even as vulnerable and fragile always potential patient. In that role, much more mixed responses, some of which have been illustrated in this book, may come into play. At this point, medical persons have no immunity. Many of these responses are wildly out of kilter with the strong, controlling and healthy scientific world-view's assumptions. Disease and healing should never be viewed only objectively and examined and treated on a scientific basis alone. Suffering and pain are always felt at a number of ambiguous and complex levels. The pastor's task is to try and bring his or her engagement with these perspectives of mixed and vulnerable attitudes to the attention of the medical establishment and institutions. The healing *may* come from the God who in the process of pain and uncertainty promotes growth and wholeness through a change of perspective.

9

Beginnings, Endings and Transitions:

Exploring death and bereavement

- **Rebecca**

I am a student teacher and I am dying. I am writing this to carers in the hope that by my telling of my story they may, some day, be better able to help those who share my experience.

I am in the hospital – I can't really remember for how long because nobody talks about such things. In fact, nobody talks about very much at all. The 'everything is all right' routine is so frustrating and makes me angry. I am left in a lonely silent void. Through the 'OK, fine' I can see the staff's own vulnerability and fear. The dying patient is a symbol of what every human person fears and what we each know: that one day we will die. I wonder what these carers do with their own feelings?

But what about my fear today and now? Endless people slip in and out of my room and give me tablets and check my blood pressure. Their fears enhance mine. Why are they afraid? I am the one who is dying.

I guess what I am saying is that it really is a question of attitude. I know we all feel insecure. I know we are all on a journey – on a search for some meaning, purpose or truth. I wish these people would stop running away – all I want to know is that there will be someone to hold my hand when I need it. I am afraid. Death may get to be a routine to them, but it's pretty new to me. I want to talk, I want to be listened to, I want to have the space to be honest about fears in a land where I know there are no answers, but only questions and anxieties.

- **James**

I am a chaplain in a hospital and I am afraid of dying. People tell me in so many different kinds of ways that they, too, are frightened of dying. So let's be honest about the shared fear, shared curiosity about life after death. I don't feel entirely comfortable with death, though in this place it is ever present. Death is part of life and part of creation; part of the cycle of birth and regeneration through death. What can I say about what death means if this fear haunts me? What can we expect from life? Are we owed a good and healthy life? Perhaps not: perhaps being human is not necessarily to be fully healthy?

• Joan

Our 24 year-old son died last year in a car accident. You don't expect, as parents, that children should beat you to the grave. We are committed Christians and I wonder whether faith has helped us on this journey. I remember reading something from Hemingway that states, 'The world breaks everyone, then some become strong at the broken places'. My own broken heart is mending and I have relearned many lessons: especially that love not only begets love, it also transmits strength. I have felt tremendous support and encouragement from others and I wonder what has helped me through.

Many things can be said when a person dies, but there is at least one thing that should never be said: 'Perhaps it was the will of God?' Why do intelligent Christians believe that God somehow goes around the world with his fingers on triggers or his hands on steering wheels? God is against all unnatural deaths. I'd rather have no meaning at all in death than this suggestion that God is somehow behind or within it.

We have had to face the bleakness, the tears and the pain. Some days are better than others. In it I believe that God has given us minimum protection and maximum support. The grief that once seemed unbearable turns to bearable sorrow. The winter has not gone but there are signs of spring.

• Robert

I am a 40 year-old accountant living with terminal cancer. The anticipation of death has made it essential for me to give thought to emotional and practical preparations for my children and my partner and parents. I have a great sense of satisfaction in having arranged for such practical matters as wills, death benefits and trust funds. For the most part this activity has been associated, not with a sense of doom or imminent death, but with a sense that making these arrangements now frees me from future concern. I need to live in the present each day, yet plan for the future and try and balance the needs of today with the uncertainties of tomorrow. Mostly, I am glad to recognize each day as a splendid unforgettable miracle, a wonderful gift to savour and enjoy as fully as I can, and when my days are no longer nourishing and good, I hope I can let go and allow myself to rest in peace.

• Kate

I am a nurse working with dying children and the aspect of my work that gives me most cause for concern is what I would describe as a 'spare me the feelings' approach to death. Modern society does not handle feelings towards death well. We act in great haste and push the reality of death as far away as possible. We want to deal with death at a safe distance, clinically and antiseptically. These attitudes seem to absolve us from the responsibility for making ourselves available to be alongside and stay in order to share some of the suffering and grief. I long for a change in our fear and ineptitude in the face of death.

★

It is hard to remain unaffected by the depth of feeling contained within the stories described above. The challenge in some ways is to integrate the experience of dying so that it can be part of all of our living and loving. The importance of an appropriate death is that dying is not an extraneous foreign process but rather a process integrated into the style, meaning and sequence of what has gone before. The challenge emerging out of these stories is how the concrete nature of all of our sense of death and dying can be appropriately integrated into our total experience.

We are a death-fearing society and our understanding of health and healing is also captive to the fear of death. It follows that the practice of medicine and nursing is influenced by such social fears and expectations. There is a process of socialization whereby many professionals can become insensitive to the reality of death. It may be true that at the end of the twentieth century death has become sanitized. In 1900 death was a common experience, many families lost children and young adults from infection, and trauma was frequent. Death occurred at home and society both accepted and adapted to it. A young man or woman in the early twenties would be most unlikely to have no experience of death and some would have been involved in the loss of many close relatives. This is not true today. Changes in medicine have come about with increasing success in combating disease which has led to cure, with little attention to the failure of medicine, as represented by death. It follows that many students emerge from medical schools with negative and deficient exposure to the universal experience of death. On qualification these young women and men are thrown into the activity of medicine where they are quite reasonably expected by the public, themselves unversed in death, to be experts in thanatology. It is little wonder, therefore, that some of the problems perceived by the stories above emerge as a direct result of the attitude of professionals to death. We all need help in coming to terms with the experience of death and dying and with learning to help others facing death for themselves or in their close relatives.

Ernest Becker (*The Denial of Death*) sees the whole of human life as an enactment of our inability to face our own mortality. He claims that we repress the sense of our death. Repression means the exclusion from consciousness of any feeling or idea, the open acknowledgment of which would be unbearably threatening or painful. It is not within the conscious control of the subject, but has destabilizing effects on the personality. It would follow then that as long as the sense of death is repressed we are, in many respects, in flight from reality, from the true self and the possibility of living a first-hand, authentic life of our own. It is a paradox that while the denial of death is endemic in humanity it turns out to be profoundly anti-life.

There is much about modern medicine that colludes with this denial of death. What is intriguing is the way in which many doctors within the context of a teaching hospital describe death, which, in part, reflects their attitude to it. It is a subject of fascination and interest as the doctor's professional skill attempts to understand the steps and process whereby the body ceases to live. This can, of course, happen by a variety of means: heart attacks and strokes; the effects of ageing and Alzheimer's disease; murder, accidents and suicide; AIDS; cancer. While it is clear that dying is a messy business, the details of death become crucially important for the doctor. They need to understand how the heart works, how the body deteriorates with age, how cancer kills. The effect of this insistence on grim detail is complex for those who work in a medicalized environment. At one level it frightens. There is the prospect one day for themselves, of pain and degradation and of being in the power of strangers. At another level, though, the effect of knowledge is more nearly that of liberation. It is as if a deep collusive silence has been broken, and there is no longer any need to pretend. Often hateful, the facts lie before you; and in acknowledging them, you are free yourself to look more squarely at the benefits life holds in store. This has contributed significantly to the culture where images of death are used unremittingly as a vehicle of entertainment, and in which death in the flesh is played down. It is also a culture in which attitudes are bizarrely quirky. The crusade against AIDS is seen as little short of holy, whereas the carnage on our roads is, for most practical purposes of prevention, ignored. This is all part of a picture of the psychology of doctors and the organization of medicine as a profession. Most of it serves to push death and dying into a corner.

Doctors have often become doctors because they are un-usually fearful of death, and as a result feel a need for control that exceeds what most people would find reasonable. Both professional pride and peace of mind become dependent on activity; and evidence, often garbled, sometimes vestigial, is used as that activity's legitimation. It follows that while passionate feelings are often expressed in the Intensive Care Unit, and tears are sometimes shed, the treatment of the terminally ill typically elicits little heartfelt concern. It also follows that patients are frequently told only that portion of the truth which makes further treatment seem reasonable.

There is a strange law of diagnosis and treatment in the organization of modern medicine today, and perhaps doctors cannot be criticized for it. The upshot is that few specialists are in a position to understand dying patients as individuals or to afford them the sympathy they require. This aspect of the culture is shared sometimes by nurses, especially within the new culture of the National Health Service. From the British standpoint, it is just such relationships of intimate trust that recent Health Service reforms, with their insistence on the costing of specific treatments within specific time frames, are rendering unsustainable.

The role of a Christian understanding of death amidst the denials, within a culture that struggles to integrate death into life, remains ambiguous and curious. It is important not to over generalize; for even with such a fact as death, personal and cultural modes of perception inescapably help to create the reality of what is perceived. Though death must be part of the human condition for always, it is not absurd to conceive of 'modern death' as very different from other experiences of this century, let alone those of the nineteenth century or mediaeval times or Japanese death. In many varied yet traditional cultures, death is always commonplace; public, terrible, ceremonial and often beautiful. The whole gamut of emotions is involved, evoked by all the varieties of dying, from public executions to domestic death in one's own bed and surrounded by one's own family. Traditional death is a significant plunge into the awful unknown, paradoxically a creative act.

Related to all this in part is the place of what comes out in the stories of many of the people above as the crisis of selfhood: 'What am I? What do I signify? Am I of value – if so to whom,

my family, to posterity or to God?' The religious dimension
obviously adds to the options and sharpens the focus. This is
where the concept of a 'good death' needs to be revived, for it
has a validity and a meaning that might help us integrate death
into life. Nowadays most people die in hospital, tucked away
behind curtains in an impersonal room, occurring probably
during a coma and, sometimes, in solitude. After death, apart
from personal grief, there is, nowadays for most people, no
public and social period of mourning comparable to what is
customary in other experiences of death. One could set our
situation against the formalities of death of former times: the
passing bell that was rung so that people could come in and bid
farewell and often to witness the death and give company to the
dying one; the last rites formally administered with sacraments
and prayers, the making of a will. Somehow modern dying,
drugged and in hospital loses so much by precluding this ethos.
The solemnity and significance of death in England is only
occasionally recognized, in the funerals of great public figures.
How acutely one felt this during the funeral of the late Labour
leader, John Smith. An egalitarian and individualistic culture
deprives the ordinary private person of any social or public
representative role, and therefore of any intrinsic general
importance. Death itself disappears from view and the fact or
act of death is no longer creative.

Sometimes great changes of feeling about the nature of things
sweep across a whole culture. For example, there is a consensus
in Western Europe that the death penalty is too harsh a
punishment for any crime, however bad. This feeling is not
accompanied by any general revulsion from or decline in
murder – rather the reverse. The level of violence in society is
rising, and in popular art death seems ever more frequent and
casual. This is all part of our modern attitude to death.

In the Christian churches we are at a curious and paradoxical
state of belief about death. The notion of Heaven as a valid
objective for personal striving is rarely presented in sermons,
and the notion of Hell is often dismissed as barbarous. Do we
believe in the resurrection of the dead or punishment beyond
death? In short, what is death? If death is conceived of as total

extinction for everyone (as it is by a large proportion of the population), it may seem at first to enhance the importance of life above all else, but in reality it does, in fact, have the reverse effect. The concept of total extinction may be true, but it removes from life the basis of all ultimate significance, all obligation, all final accountability. If death is extinction for everyone, it has no significance: in so far as death loses significance, so does life. Hence the trivialization of both life and death in much of ordinary culture and the nihilism of much contemporary art. The effects throughout our culture are enormous. Modern angst and modern concepts of death depend upon, perhaps arise out of, freedom, individuality and prosperity. We feel that freedom, individualism and prosperity are intrinsically good. They are undoubtedly imperilled by the nihilism and irrationality which accompany them. In order to preserve the good things which we value in this life, the most important achievement then that we can hope for in religious, and thus in social and political terms, would be the development or recreation of generally acceptable belief in some other life, or personal survival beyond death. Such a belief, perhaps, can restore the terrors and the creativity of our notion of death, and so give us a basis for seeing significance in this life. However it might be envisaged, the stories described to us above call out for a development of an art of death and dying. Such an art would need to take proper account of our dignity, our relationships and our achievements. We all have a 'place in history'. It needs recognition as we leave its stage.

The role of those who stand by and accompany people who die is an important and crucial one. There is much evidence to suggest a crippling level of role uncertainty for many professional Christians within this situation. Often the role has been marginalized unless the person in question has attempted to become a professional amongst professionals. Techniques and skills informed by social sciences are of vital importance, but they are not in themselves Christian skills and there is nothing in their fundamental character which makes the one practising them recognizable as one proclaiming the gospel. In fact what makes the carer a good carer is not what they may or may not believe, but their level of competence as a professional and their qualities as a human being. Perhaps the role is one of friendship, of self-disclosure, of the sharing of questions and feelings; of a dying person speaking to a dying person, attempting to integrate this experience of dying from whatever perspective, into loving and living. The Christian carer must offer these qualities at the very least.

Throughout this encounter with illness there are many common strands in the stories which have been examined: coming clean and facing facts honestly; the encounter with suffering, pain and loss; drawing close to people and trying to help and, above all, confronting the reality and finality of our mortality, and being able to be weak and vulnerable. There is one key thread which is easy to miss in our death-denying society. We are perhaps conditioned to avoid confronting fear, to avoid the wilderness, the desert places in our own hearts and world. We live under what some have called the tyranny of certainty, where apparent strength, confidence, life and security dominate our emotional and ecclesiastical lives. In the quest for healing, we seek those things that reassure us rather than those things which confront our doubts and fears. The individuals whose stories are shared with us ask us to think about how meaning is part of our lives and, above all, where our security and strength lie. Fearful Christians build fearful Christian communities, where uncertainty, contradiction, paradox and ambiguity are masked by false security, apparent strength and a façade of certainty. The integration of living our experience of dying means facing our own and each other's vulnerability. In some senses, when we are vulnerable there can be healing and growth as we accept our need of others, and when we let go of our independence and of our drive to assert. The gospel, in this and other contexts, demands that we are drawn out of the tyranny of certainty, to be powerful through our giving and to be vulnerable through our receiving as we hold together the paradoxes and contradictions between life and death, faith and fear, hope and despair, loving and hating, alienation and relationship, fragmentation and connectedness.

Perhaps the role of our Christian faith and commitment is

more problematical. It is possible to become so accustomed to the starkness of the imagery and meaning of Christian symbols that they lose the power to challenge and confront us. Too often our religion opts for purity, clarity and distance. At the heart of faith is the death of Jesus and its power to create new life, to transform both life and death, but it is in essence a mystery. This death and our deaths are a mystery. The meaning of mystery is not a truth so great that we are not required to have an understanding of it, but a truth so deep that our understandings will be insufficient to understand the whole. Peter Harvey speaks of the gospel message as offering us certain promise only of uncertainty, of continuing loss and change. He reminds us that comprehending mystery is the process of recognizing not of *what* we do not know, but *that* we do not know. The integration of our experience of dying is engaging with the struggle to manage the profound paradoxes and ambiguities as a condition of our living.

Perhaps there is much about human experience, including the encounter with illness, that make it difficult to believe in a God that unfolds to us a picture of our world as a friendly and meaningful place. The world, for many, is a process in which one feels alienated, engulfed and lost. But it is into that process that God comes and speaks to us. The only liturgy that God gave is the liturgy in which death is celebrated. So the pastor must confront this. What is it like to be dead? All of us know a little about it. We know how hard transitions away from home can be, the pain of separation, of those small losses and changes which make up our lives. And there are many signs of the times that indicate the place of death in our world. What does the possession of nuclear bombs tell us about ourselves? The bomb, surely, is the fruit of repression – our naive belief that death does not really exist, that the human race must be assured of life forever, in a world where there will be no end. Our possession of these weapons arises from and intensifies this illusion, while at the same time threatening the world with unprecedented catastrophe. Perhaps it is our own anxiety which makes us so mistrustful of our feelings, a life that refuses to accept the reality of life in us and around us.

The gospel offers us an alternative to this repressed sense of death. We are shown in a particular death a capacity for offered suffering and are invited to live in its light. This is what we have to offer others as we attempt to live out this truth in our lives. So it is that we should want to resist anything that denies death, for when it is denied it casts a shadow over all our projects; it threatens our whole life's course with the lack of meaning. God's promise and invitation is available in and through loss: there has to be surrender, even the risking of intimacy with God. We need, therefore, to become less strong, less confident, less and less defended, less and less identified with our own ideas of God and more attentive to the promptings of the Spirit and to the other person's story.

Perhaps this is what those who share their story about illness teach us: that we have to accept our loss and death in the unfolding and discovering of the capacity to live our own lives in all their pain and complexity.

Encountering Illness:
Conclusions – areas for further thought and pastoral reflection

What happens can never be anticipated. What happens escapes anything you can ever say about it. What happens cannot be undone. It can never be anything other than it is. We tell stories as if to refuse this truth, as if to say that we make our fate, rather than simply endure it. But in truth we make nothing. We live, and we cannot shape life. It is much too great for us, too great for any words. A writer must refuse to believe this, must believe there is nothing that cannot somehow be said. Yet there at last in her presence, in the unending unfolding of that silence, which still goes on, which I still expect to be broken by another drawing in of breath, I knew that all my words could only be in vain, and that all that I feared and all that I had anticipated could only be lived – without their help or hers.

Michael Ignatieff, *Scar Tissue* (p. 172)

Below my window in Ross, when I'm working in Ross, for example, at this season, the blossom is out in full now . . . it's a plum tree, it looks like apple blossom but it's white, and looking at it, instead of saying, 'Oh that's nice blossom' . . . Last week looking at it through the window when I'm writing, I *see* it is the whitest, frothiest, blossomest blossom there ever could be, and I can see it. Things are both more trivial than they ever were, and more important than they ever were, and the difference between the trivial and the important doesn't seem to matter. But the nowness of everything is absolutely wondrous, and if people could *see* that, you know. There is no way of telling you, you have to experience it, but the glory of if, if you like the comfort of it, the reassurance . . . The fact is, if you see the present tense, boy do you see it! And boy can you celebrate it.

Dennis Potter, *Seeing the Blossom: Two Interviews and a Lecture* (p. 5)

Consider the following now.
One. Illness. Not the beginning of the end but the beginning of THE beginning. To be honest I did not FEEL this very strongly till about six months ago. Nevertheless, I lived everyday since my diagnosis to the fullest knowing physical exertion would speed the progression of the illness. To sit back, however, would only have robbed me of moments with my family and friends.

Thus I continue. Only now I sense if I had become a stoic or a fighter, I would have probably been gone by now. Rather, I face each day with a prayer. I try to be completely open to whatever Christ brings.

Scar Tissue (p. 130)

Michael Ignatieff explores the world of illness with the power and force of a novelist's skill. At the heart of *Scar Tissue* is a son's account of his mother's voyage into a world of neurological disease, losing her memory and then her very identity, only to gain at the very end a strange serenity. The son in the novel, who is obsessed with his mother's transformation sets out on his own quest for self-discovery. What can be said of illness and how do the intellectual and the emotional belong together? Should we regard illness as meaningful in any kind of way? And, in the end, what ever is said, perhaps we will never be able either to anticipate what happens or to explain it.

The piece from Dennis Potter's interview with Melvyn Bragg a few months before he died is a moving and powerful statement about one person's experience of the transformation of perspective through terminal disease. It is a testimony of how death changes seeing and knowing in life. It is also a reflection of the paradoxical nature of the relationship between the quantity and the quality of our lives and living.

Somehow these two perspectives need to be held together. Illness is both meaningful and meaningless. The voices of illness can say many things to us as we face the ambiguity of disease and its message to society and the individual's relationship within it. Meaning is often ambiguous and words work in different ways. Perhaps the body speaks a particular kind of language through the functioning of its organs, and even expresses something of the essence or the soul of humanity. So illness is connected with the whole variety of aspects of life. Illness is both alienation and communication, and it is the source of many and conflicting values. We must continue to ask whether every event has a cause and in what way our inner and outer worlds are linked.

Yet amidst all this there is an essential loneliness or unspokenness about illness. The pastoral attempt at solidarity with the sick is not always respectful of the immense solitude of those who find themselves ill. Illness takes them into a foreign country; and it tests the already limited ability of humans to put themselves in each other's skins, to empathize with them through shared memories of the same condition.

Above all, in the encounter with illness what is required is honesty and attention: honesty in the engagement with experience and attention to the sheer diversity of voices and influences which shape that experience. In the introduction to Dennis Potter's interview, *Seeing the Blossom*, Melvyn Bragg shares his anxiety in anticipating his encounter with Potter, and in doing so shares the following advice which is a powerful paradigm for modern Christian pastoral care:

The main problem as far as I was concerned was to avoid mawkishness, sentimentality or any whisper of the wrong sort of intrusiveness, or any sort of intrusiveness. The main purpose that I had was to give him as much space and time and energy as possible for as long as possible (p. xi).

Bragg succeeds in so far as he allows Potter to articulate his experience and what shapes it with richness, profundity and meaning.

Appendix

Source material
and
suggestions for further reading

Introduction

Paul H. Ballard (ed.), *The Foundations of Pastoral Studies and Practical Theology*, Holi-4, Faculty of Theology, Cardiff 1986

Wesley Carr, *The Pastor as Theologian: The Integration of Pastoral Ministry, Theology and Discipleship*, SPCK 1989

David Deeks, *Pastoral Theology: An Enquiry*, Epworth 1987

Elaine Graham and Margaret Halsey (eds), *Life Cycles: Women and Pastoral Care*, SPCK 1993

Laurie Green, *Lets Do Theology: A Pastoral Cycle Resource Book*, Mowbray 1990

Lewis S. Mudge and James N. Poling (eds), *The Promise of Practical Theology: Formation and Reflection*, Fortress, Philadelphia 1987

Stephen Pattison, *A Critique of Pastoral Care*, SCM Press 1988

John Patton, *From Ministry to Theology: Pastoral Action and Reflection*, Abingdon Press, Nashville 1990

Michael Wilson, *A Coat of Many Colours: Pastoral Studies of the Christian Way of Life*, Epworth 1988

James Woodward (ed.), *Embracing The Chaos: Theological Responses to AIDS*, SPCK 1990

1. Pain, Loss and Anxiety: Exploring human existence in the light of illness

Nigel Collinson and David Matthews (eds), *Facing Illness*, Epworth 1986

Hilton Davis and Lesley Fallowfield (eds), *Counselling and Communication in Health Care*, Wiley 1993

Ray Fitzpatrick, John Hinton, Stanton Newman, Graham Scambler, James Thompson, *The Experience of Illness*, Tavistock 1984

George Peter Murdock, *Theories of Illness: A World Survey*, University of Pittsburgh 1980

Philip Myerscough, *Talking with Patients: A Basic Clinical Skill*, OUP 1990

James O'Conner, *The Meaning of Crisis: A Theoretical Introduction*, Blackwell 1987

Paul Tillich, *The Courage To Be*, Penguin 1952

2. Waiting, Watching and Hoping: Exploring the perspectives of relatives and friends

Norman Autton, *Pain: An Exploration*, DLT 1986

Mary Louise Bringle, *Despair, Sickness or Sin? Hopelessness and Healing in the Christian Life*, Abingdon, Nashville 1990

Mary Craig, interview with Dennis Potter, in *The Listener*, December 1981

Jessie van Dongen-Garrad, *Invisible Barriers*, SPCK 1983

Regis Duffy, *A Roman Catholic Theology of Pastoral Care*, Fortress Press, Philadelphia 1983

Michael Jacobs, *Towards the Fullness of Christ: Pastoral Care and Christian Maturity*, DLT 1988

Michael Jacobs, *Still Small Voice*, SPCK 1982

John V. Taylor, *The Go-between God*, SCM Press 1972

John V. Taylor, *The Christ-like God*, SCM Press 1992

W. H. Vanstone, *The Stature of Waiting*, DLT 1982

Leslie Virgo (ed.), *First Aid in Pastoral Care*, T. and T. Clark 1987

Robert Wuthnow, *Acts of Compassion: Caring for Others and Helping Ourselves*, Princeton University Press 1991

3. Myths, Meanings and Re-evaluations: Exploring coping mechanisms in illness

Charles A. Corr and Donna M. Corr (eds), *Hospice Care: Principles and Practice*, Faber & Faber 1983

R. J. Dunlop and J. M. Hockley, *Terminal Care Support Teams: The Hospital – Hospice Interface*, OUP 1990

Tom Heller, Lorna Bailey and Stephen Pattison (eds), *Preventing Cancers*, Open University Press 1992

Raymond Hitchcock, *Fighting Cancer: A Personal Story*, Angel 1989

Michael Jacobs (ed.), *Faith or Fear? A Reader in Pastoral Care and Counselling*, DLT 1987

Ivan Lichter, *Communication in Cancer Care*, Churchill Livingstone 1988

Stirling Moorey and Steven Greer, *Psychological Therapy for Patients with Cancer: A New Approach*, Heinemann 1989

Peter Speck, *Being There: Pastoral Care in Time of Illness*, SPCK 1988

4. Stigma, Prejudice and Projections: Exploring illness as a social and cultural reality

Louis Abbleby, *A Medical Tour Through the Whole Island of Great Britain*, Faber & Faber 1994

Alan Brandt, *No Magic Bullet: A Social History of Venereal Disease in the United States since 1880*, OUP 1987

Mary Douglas, *Purity and Danger: An Analysis of the Concepts of Pollution and Taboo*, Ark 1994

Saunders Gillman, *Disease and Representation: Images of Illness from Madness to AIDS*, Cornell University Press 1988

Cindy Pattern, *Sex and Germs: The Politics of AIDS*, Southend Press, Boston 1985

Simon Watney, *Policing Desire: Pornography, Aids and the Media*, Comedia/Methuen 1987

Geoffrey Weeks, *Sexuality and Its Discontents: Meaning, Myths and Modern Sexualities*, Routledge 1985

James Woodward, *Representation and Practice in the Pastoral Care of People Living with Human Immunodeficiency Virus and Acquired Immune Deficiency Syndrome* (unpublished Master of Philosophy Thesis), The University of Birmingham 1991

5. Separation, Alienation and Powerlessness: Exploring experiences of pastoral care

David Lyall, *Counselling in the Pastoral and Spiritual Context*, Open University Press 1995

Jeffrey Masson, *Against Therapy*, Fontana 1988

Dorothy Rowe, *Beyond Fear*, Fontana 1987

Dorothy Rowe, *The Construction of Life and Death: Discovering Meaning in a World of Uncertainty*, Fontana 1982

David Smail, *Allusion and Reality: The Meaning of Anxiety*, Dent & Sons 1984

David Smail, *Taking Care: An Alternative to Therapy*, Dent & Sons 1987

Neville Symington, *Emotion and Spirit: Questioning the Claims of Psychoanalysis and Religion*, Mowbray 1994

Frank Wright, *Pastoral Care for Lay People*, SCM Press 1982

Frank Wright, *Pastoral Nature of the Ministry*, SCM Press 1980

6. Decisions, Dilemmas and Choices: Exploring patient autonomy, ethics and options in illness

J. M. Bell and S. Mendus (eds), *Philosophy and Medical Welfare*, Cambridge University Press 1988

Alastair Campbell, Grant Gillett and Gareth Jones, *Practical Medical Ethics*, OUP 1992

A. S. Duncan, G. R. Dunstan, R. B. Welbourne (eds), *Dictionary of Medical Ethics*, DLT 1981

K. W. M. Fulford, Grant Gillett and Janet Martin Soskice, *Medical and Moral Reasoning*, CUP 1995

Carol Gilligan, *In A Different Voice*, Harvard 1988

John Harris, *The Value Of Life*, Routledge 1985

Ian Kennedy, *Treat Me Right*, OUP 1988

J. F. Kilner, *Who Lives Who Dies?* Yale University Press 1990

Alan Maynard, 'Logic in medicine: an economic perspective', *BMJ* 1987, p. 295

Peter Singer (ed.), *Applied Ethics*, CUP 1986

The British Medical Association's, Ethics, Science and Information Division, *Medical Ethics Today: Its Practice and Philosophy*, BMJ 1993

A. Williams, 'Cost effectiveness analysis: is it ethical?', *Journal of Medical Ethics*, 1992, p. 18

7. Caring, Curing and Learning: Exploring the agencies and institutions of health care

Nick Black, David Boswell, Alastair Gray, Shaun Murphy and Jenny Popay (eds), *Health and Disease: A Reader*, Open University Press 1984

Eliot Freidson, *Professor Of Medicine*, Dodd, Mead & Co, New York 1975

Christopher Ham, *Health Policy in Britain*, Macmillan 1992

P. D. James, *The Children of Men*, Faber & Faber 1994

Linda Jones, *The Social Context of Health and Healthwork*, Macmillan 1994

Ian Kennedy, *The Unmasking of Medicine*, Allen & Unwin 1981

Rudolf Klein, *The Politics of the NHS*, Longman 1989

Thomas McKeown, *The Role of Medicine*, Blackwell 1979

Roy Porter, *Disease, Medicine and Society in England 1550–1860*, Macmillan 1987

Margaret Stacey, *The Sociology of Health and Healing*, Unwin Hyman 1988

The Open University, Department of Health and Social Welfare, *K258 Health and Wellbeing*, 1993

8. Divine Action, Prayer and Belief: Exploring the hope and possibility of healing

Austin Farrer, *Love Almighty and Ills Unlimited*, Collins 1962

David Jenkins, *God, Miracle and the Church of England*, SCM Press 1988

Morris Maddocks, *The Christian Healing Ministry*, SPCK 1981

Stephen Parsons, *The Challenge of Christian Healing*, SPCK 1986

Stephen Pattison, *Alive and Kicking*, SCM Press 1989

John Polkinghorne, *Science and Christian Belief*, SPCK 1994

Richard Swinburne, *The Concept of Miracle*, Macmillan 1970

Maurice Wiles, *God's Action in the World*, SCM Press 1986

Michael Wilson, *The Church is Healing*, SCM Press 1967

Michael Wilson, *Health is for People*, DLT 1975

Frank Wright, *The Pastoral Nature of Healing*, SCM Press 1985

9. Beginnings, Endings and Transitions: Exploring death and bereavement

Ray S. Anderson, *Theology, Death and Dying*, Blackwell 1986

Peter Berger, *A Rumour of Angels*, Penguin 1971

John Bowker, *Problems of Suffering in Religions of the World*, CUP 1970

Sheila Cassidy, *Light from the Dark Valley: Reflections on Suffering in the Care of the Dying*, DLT 1994

Sheila Cassidy, *Sharing the Darkness*, DLT 1988

Paul Fiddes, *The Creative Suffering of God*, Clarendon 1988

Nicholas Peter Harvey, *Death's Gift*, Epworth 1985

Sebastion Moore, *The Inner Loneliness*, DLT 1982

Colin Murray Parkes, *Bereavement*, Penguin 1979
Henri Nouwen, *In Memoriam*, Ave Maria Press 1990
Averil Stedeford, *Facing Death*, Sobell Publications 1994
Margaret Spufford, *Celebration*, Collins 1989

10. Encountering Illness: Conclusions – areas for further thought and pastoral reflection

Michael Ignatieff, *Scar Tissue*, Vintage 1994
Dennis Potter, *Seeing the Blossom*, Faber & Faber 1994